# MOCKTAIL COO[

*365 DAYS OF COLORFUL AND REFRESHING NON-ALCOHOLIC DRINK RECIPES TO TRY AT HOME*

Anais Khan

# Table of Contents

# Introduction

Mocktails come in handy at gatherings with friends and family. Even just imagining them makes the atmosphere festive. The recipes are so straightforwardly basic that you won't have a hard time making them. Another benefit is that mocktails are deliciously efficient – they may be created quickly and without much effort. Most mocktail recipes call on fruits and juices, making them quite healthy drinks. The nicest thing about mocktails is how well they keep you energized and alert. They don't make you feel hot or raise your body temperature like hard alcoholic drinks or cocktails do.

Consequently, you avoid the inconvenience of perspiring while drinking them. The fruity flavor combinations never let anyone down. In actuality, drinkers of all ages genuinely like mocktails. Most people have favorite mocktails that they frequently order or create themselves. So, what're you still holding out for? Go ahead and make one for yourself using the recipes in this cookbook!

Non-alcoholic beverages called mocktails imitate the flavors and presentation of cocktails. Mocktails and cocktails are fundamentally different in that mocktails lack alcohol, while cocktails often contain at least one form of spirit.

Mocktails can be made using a variety of components, including soda, herbs, and spices. Some unique creations can stand alone, while others resemble unadulterated versions of well-known cocktails. A lot of mocktails have fruit or other garnishes and are vibrantly colored.

A mocktail typically has a diverse flavor profile that balances savory, sweet, and sour flavors. They are popular among designated drivers, expectant mothers, and individuals who abstain from alcohol for various reasons. People of all ages can enjoy them.

There is bound to be a recipe to fit your taste, whether you're looking for a cool summer drink or a joyful holiday mocktail.

Learning about the development of mocktails and their popularity is fascinating. Although mocktails have been around for centuries, the American public first became familiar with them during the Prohibition era. People experimented with ways to make their favorite Mocktails without using spirits because alcohol was prohibited.

Mocktails remained popular over the years, but they have recently seen a comeback as more consumers seek out non-alcoholic alternatives to their favorite flavors.

You'll need a few ingredients if you want to make your mocktails at home.

In contrast to cocktails, making mocktails is comparable to cooking. Mix your berries and fruits planted in your backyard with other ingredients to make a delicious mocktail. Mocktails can also be made with vegetables. You can use sweeteners like agave, simple syrup, or honey. To make a fantastic bubbly drink, add soda water.

Start now!

# Chapter 1: Tools and Glasses

## Blender

One may already exist in your kitchen, but if not, you'll need a decent blender for some of these drinks, particularly the ones where you'll have to make purees or otherwise break down good amounts of fruit, vegetables, or crushed ice. A 32-ounce blender should do the trick.

It's amazing nowadays how wildly blenders range in price - anywhere from twenty bucks to over four hundred dollars! You want something that's got enough power, especially for pulverizing ice, but you don't need one that's got the propulsion of a fighter jet. You'll also pay a lot for the design, and while a sleek and fancy blender is pretty to look at, especially those cool retro ones, it's not crucial to pay big bucks, mainly if you're operating on a budget. You should be able to get a great, long-lasting blender from a reputable company for somewhere around forty or fifty bucks.

## Mocktail Shaker

You absolutely will need a Mocktail shaker. You can get a couple of varieties — pros may favor a Boston shaker, a two-piece device you can use together for shaking or separately when you're muddling or stirring. You'll need a filter, too, unless you're so good that you can strain through a razor-thin gap you make between the two pieces after you're done shaking. But that takes a lot of practice, trust me. It's not as easy as it looks! It's certainly impressive once you get good at it. A word of caution: a newbie with a Boston shaker is a disaster. Your drinks very well may go everywhere except the glass!

What you'll probably want is what's called a cobbler shaker. You can find them just about anywhere glassware and dishware are sold. They're three parts: the shaker, a strainer, and a lid. They're incredibly easy to use. No mess, although the only downside to a cobbler shaker over a Boston shaker is that sometimes the parts can be a little tricky to separate when you're making your drink once everything gets cold, something about vacuums and so forth (I'm no scientist, sorry!). However, once you make a few drinks with it, you'll figure out how to make it work, and it won't be a problem. They're also a little bit more of a pain to clean than a Boston shaker, but the convenience of use makes up for that. Bottom line: if you're not a seasoned drink maker, go with the cobbler shaker. You should be able to find a shaker for between five and twenty bucks.

# Collins

You'll want Collins glasses (also called "highball glasses" or "chimney glasses") which are taller and skinnier than tumblers yet just as essential. You'll usually find them in the 10-ounce to 16-ounce range. They're great for fizzier drinks, many of which you'll find in this book. I'd recommend going with the 12-ounce Collins glasses.

# Copper Mug

As you've undoubtedly heard, Moscow mules have become all the rage in the Mocktail world in recent years, and copper mugs are simply the best vessel to drink them, mainly since they'll keep your drink icy cold on hot summer days. The mule variation mocktail recipe found in this book is no exception. Copper mugs are rad. Get some.

# Coupe

Coupe glasses are my absolute favorite glass in the whole world! They're elegant, sexy, classic, and so much fun to drink out of. They're stemmed like a Mocktail glass but shallower and more saucer- or bowl-like. They're often found in 5.5-ounce and 6-ounce sizes. They're interchangeable with traditional

Mocktail /martini glasses. You can also use them instead of the tall, thin champagne flutes, which are classic but not nearly as versatile.

## Flute

As mentioned earlier, they're tall, thin, stemmed, dainty, and traditionally used for champagne. They're certainly nice to have, and it wouldn't be right to steer clear from them, but you could use a coupe glass instead.

## Glassware

Not getting around it — you'll need many different kinds of glasses. Fortunately, they're inexpensive and should last a while, provided you're not super klutzy and dropping them on the kitchen floor all the time.

## Hurricane

Made to look like old-school hurricane lamps, hurricane glasses are tall and kind of pear-shaped or vase-like (or, if you like, narrow in the waist and a little wider at the top and the bottom like a real woman!). They're great for blended and frozen drinks — and there are many such recipes in this book — and you can typically find them in 15-ounce and 20-ounce sizes, both of which are recommended.

## Juicer

As mentioned earlier, if you use fresh juices in your drinks instead of bottled juices, your mocktails will taste a lot better. So, while it's not mandatory by any means, it's recommended you get a juicer. Like blenders, prices range wildly. The high-end ones are awesome, powerful, and easy to clean, but they're expensive — you can pay a couple of hundred bucks for those. I've had the juicer I bought at a big-box department store for sixty bucks for ten years now, and it's never let me down. It's a pain to clean, but it works like a charm, and having one makes all the difference in the world between just "okay" drinks and fantastic drinks!

# Knives/Openers

Assuming you already have a couple of sharp knives and a bottle opener in your kitchen, if you want separate knives and openers for your Mocktail set-up, then, by all means, do it. But you can let the ones you already have do double-duty. Keep your knives sharp, though! You'll need them for slicing lemons, limes, and other citrus fruits. If you don't already have a peeler/zester, you should get one of those, especially for making garnishes out of lemon or lime peels. You should be able to find a good one for under ten dollars because they are not pricey.

# Measuring Devices

After making drinks for a while, you can eyeball liquid amounts, but even the pros need assistance from time to time, and novices need something to measure out juices, syrups, and other ingredients. For a small sum, you can obtain a shot glass with measurements on the side or a standard metal double jigger that's 1 ounce on one end and ½ ounce on the other. They're easy and fun to use. However, if you have to measure out something like 1 ¼ ounce, you'd have to guesstimate a little, but they make slightly more expensive double jiggers with marked increments like those shot glasses. Also, you'll want the usual measuring cups and spoons, which you probably already have in your kitchen, maybe stuffed in a drawer somewhere.

# Mesh Strainers

It's just so handy to have a set of stainless steel fine-mesh strainers with handles in different sizes. You'll always use them, and they're pretty cheap and super-durable. You can usually get a set of three filters in 3-inch, 5-inch, and 8-inch diameters for ten bucks or less.

# Muddler

Several recipes here require "muddling" ingredients like herbs, fruits, spices, and berries in a shaker or glass. Muddling is simply a fancy way of saying you're going to mash those ingredients with a device called a muddler so that you can release their flavors, and your drinks will taste extra delicious. Now, you can likely get away with utilizing a wooden spoon you probably have in your kitchen (most beginners do that at first). Some say, however, that that practice leaves undesirable residue in your beverage. You can get a 10-inch stainless steel muddler with a head made out of nylon for around eight bucks; it'll do a great job — the length and weight of it are perfect. You can find fancy muddlers for over twenty or twenty-five bucks, but that isn't necessary.

# Pitcher

You'll want a couple of large, sturdy glass pitchers for several of the recipes in this book. Try not to get anything too heavy, though, since they'll already be holding lots of liquid. Stick with glass pitchers, too, over plastic ones.

# Punch Bowl

You'll want at least one good-sized glass punch bowl for entertaining larger gatherings.

A few notes about glasses: you can spend a little to a whole lot on them when you buy them new. What you prefer to spend is up to you. It's not recommended to get thin glasses for your mocktails, though. Go for the sturdier glassware. Additionally, one of the finest places to find glassware is your local thrift store. You can always find amazing glassware there for cheap. Just ensure you check for cracks, chips, and whatnot. You'll need a lot of glasses of various kinds to do entertaining right, but you can find great glassware pretty cheap.

# Tumbler

First, you'll need some tumblers (a.k.a. "rocks glasses," "lowball glasses", or "old-fashioned glasses"). You'll want 10-ounce tumblers for versatility, and it's also recommended to get the thicker-bottomed ones because not only are they better for muddling in the glass when necessary, but their weight feels good and exactly right in the hand. Many times, with drinks served in tumblers, you'll be making the drink right in the tumbler, so you'll want something durable and sturdy.

# Wine Glass

Some of the drinks in this book call for a wine glass, so it's always good to have red wine and white wine glasses around. White wine glasses are somewhat narrower and squatter than red wine glasses.

# Chapter 2: Ingredients & Preparations

Generally, the better the quality of the ingredients you use to make your drinks, the better they will taste and look. Obvious, right? However, this doesn't mean you have to empty your wallet. You don't necessarily need that super-fancy ten-dollar tonic water bottle at your local specialty store - the 79-cent two-liter bottle at the supermarket will do more than fine. Hey, if you have the big bucks and want to splurge, go for it! But if you're living on an average person's budget, go the cheaper route on things like tonic water and club soda.

Generally speaking, if you have a juicer (we'll talk about some essential mocktail tools in the next section) and can make fresh orange juice or fresh vegetable juices, that would be ideal. There is still hope if you don't have a juicer. Many supermarkets carry fresh orange juice, fresh pineapple juice, and even fresh mango and papaya juices, although they can certainly get pricy. Just try to get the highest quality bottled juices that you can afford. There are one or two recipes in this book where you can get away with using frozen juice concentrate, but for the most part, you should steer clear of that.

As for melons, bananas, peaches, and other fruits that you'll be putting into a blender for various drinks, or perhaps berries that you'll be muddling or using as a garnish, make sure they're ripe but not overripe. It's not an exact science, but sometimes when the fruit is overripe, it will affect your drink's final flavor.

One big truth of mastering the art of the rockin' mocktail is that it's not necessarily the making of the drink that'll make you shine but the careful and wise selection of the ingredients beforehand. Finding fruits and vegetables at the peak of ripeness pays well. Everyone has their techniques - some people in the supermarket tap on their melons and thoroughly inspect their plums. They may seem like crazy people sometimes, but they have more power if they're getting the best ones available! When in doubt, ask someone in your local produce department for help. Or befriend a farmer! When everything else fails, you should be able to at least get assistance from the internet.

When it comes to herbs in these recipes, whether mixed into the drink or used as a garnish, fresh is the only way. Please don't use dried herbs! You will not be happy if you do. I highly recommend growing your herbs — mint especially, basil and sage — once spring approaches. You can put them on a window sill, on your stoop, or in the backyard; it's cheap and fun! Many of the mocktails in this book call for mint. Mint is your friend. Grow some! But hey, if you're a brown thumb, the good news is that herbs like mint and basil are available at just about any supermarket and are inexpensive.

If you're someone who swears by only organic fruits and vegetables, go for it. There aren't many people like you, especially since organic produce can be expensive. Honestly, though, most people don't think it makes that much of a difference when it comes to your drink at the end of the day, but again, if it's something you already do or want to do, just do it!

A couple of other things before we move on to the tools of the trade. You're not going to find too many exotic ingredients in this book. Everything ought to be rather simple to locate in your area or to access online. Invest in a bottle or two of aromatic bitters (like angostura bitters), grenadine syrup, and other flavored syrups that aren't easily made at home. Drinks that call for bitters usually require only a dash or two, so your bottle will last a while, and bitters add so much to many drinks. It's kind of amazing how they can elevate a drink. A critical note about bitters: bitters contain exceedingly small amounts of alcohol, though the amount the recipes in this book call for (usually a dash or two) will add a virtually negligible amount of alcohol to your drink. However, if you or the people you are serving your mocktails to are abstaining from alcohol totally and completely and cannot consume even the tiniest amount — for religious reasons, for example — then you should steer clear of the recipes that call for bitters.

Changing gears... This cookbook has numerous recipes that call for simple syrup. In each recipe that calls for it, there are provided amounts to make a decent-sized batch of simple syrup to use and store the rest. Still, if you already have some in the fridge from another one of the many recipes in this book, you don't have to make another full batch (still, it couldn't hurt — it's cheap, easy, and great to have on hand all the time).

Another crucial point here: while most of the drinks in this book can be made pretty fast, especially if you're just flipping through the pages for something new and find a recipe you want to make right now, a few of the recipes require some preparation, whether it's making a flavored syrup ahead of time and allowing it to cool, or steeping teas or coffees or other ingredients before you get to mixing (sometimes for several hours or even overnight). Be sure to read through the recipe, so you don't get stuck without the necessary components right before your party begins!

One last incredibly crucial piece of advice in this section: you cannot have enough ice! Especially if you are hosting a party. Make or buy lots and lots and lots of ice! It's cheap; you'll need and use it! You'll be hatin' it if you run out, so make sure you have more than you think you'll need on hand (and somewhere to keep it!).

# Chapter 3: Techniques

## Building

Often, this is how mocktails and most other drinks are made. When using this method, all ingredients are directly poured into and mixed in the glass they are to be served in. You will use this method whenever you see "build-in glass" or something similar in a recipe in the book.

## Straining

Any strain that can stop the ice and particles of fruit created from stirring and shaking will do the job. However, if you're looking around the market for a dedicated strainer, you might want to get a hawthorn strainer or a julep strainer. Hawthorn strainers are great for straining a shaken drink, and a Julep strainer is great for a stirred drink.

# Fine Straining/Double Straining

Sometimes, we want to get ultra-clear drinks. Super small particles of fruit sometimes pass through the hawthorn and julep strainers. In this case, straining the drink a second time using a super fine strainer might be helpful. Any fine sieve, like a tea strainer, will do the job.

# Blending

A few recipes in this book will ask you to do something along the lines of "blend with ice." In these recipes, you pour all ingredients into a blender, then put the ice in it and blend until a uniform, smooth consistency is achieved. For these recipes, crushed ice works best because it makes the blender's job much simpler.

# Throwing

Throwing is the process of pouring ingredients from one container into another container from a height. This causes the cascading liquid to pull air into the drink. With the process, greater dilution and aeration are achieved compared to the stirring process.

To elaborate, you will first need to pour all ingredients into your shaker and add ice. Next, you will strain the mixture into a second container. Ensure the second container has a large opening and a lipped rim to avoid spilling. As you pour, you will increase the distance between the two containers. Next, pour the liquid from the second container back into the ice-filled first container. Repeat this multiple times, and you will have a "thrown" drink.

# Rolling

Rolling is like shaking but much gentler. To do this, fill your Mocktail shaker with the ingredients and gently roll it end to end. This process is used in drinks like the Bloody Mary, where the thick texture needs to be maintained.

# Swizzling

Swizzling is simply stirring using a swizzling stick. Hold the rod of the swizzling stick between the palms of both your hands while the stick is immersed in the drink, and rotate the stick back and forth rapidly by sliding your hands.

# Layering

The coolest-looking drinks are made using the layering method. Drinks prepared this way have the ingredients - usually of contrasting colors - floating one over the other.

You will need to be cautious while preparing drinks using this technique because it only works when the density of the ingredients varies considerably. Generally, ingredients with more sugar and less alcohol are denser. So, when layering, the heaviest ingredient is poured in first, and the lightest ingredient is poured in last.

Syrups, for instance, have no alcohol and a lot of sugar. These ingredients are, therefore, heavy and poured in first. Liqueurs, which are higher in sugar and lower in alcohol than spirits, usually come after the syrups, and spirits come last. It will be the topmost ingredient if the recipe uses a creamy liqueur.

# Shaking

You may find a few recipes in this book that say, "shake with ice and strain." In such recipes, you must quickly shake all the components, including the ice cubes, in a mocktail shaker. Don't hold back. Give the shake all you've got. Shake for approximately 15 seconds, then strain the mixture into the glass you wish to serve it in. Make sure the ice stays behind in the strain.

This method cools, dilutes, and aerates the drink, all at the same time. The more you shake, the greater the dilution and cooling achieved, so you can shake following your preferences.

As a general guideline, fill the shaker with ice to a depth of 60–70%. Also, be careful your hand doesn't

slip while shaking, as there are quite a few ultra-smooth Mocktail shakers on the market. Holding and shaking with two hands might not seem as "cool" is doing it with one hand, but it is the safer way to do it. But in the end, it'll just be you, so go ahead and do it your way!

# Dry Shake

For this technique, instead of giving all the ingredients and ice one good mix, we will first shake the ingredients without ice. This way, they'll combine more easily thanks to the slightly high temperature. After that, ice is added, and the beverage is shaken once more to cool and dilute it.

# Stirrers and Stirring

This is the same technique we use to dissolve sugar in a hot cup of coffee, but in the case of a Mocktail, you might need to do it with a little more zeal.

You will do well to grab a dedicated stirring glass. These lipped glasses come in all shapes and sizes and are easily available on amazon. Next, you will need a tool to stir the mixture with. Any long spoon will do the trick if you do not wish to be stylish. You can grab a bat teaspoon if you like to host fancy parties or just want to stir with style in front of your friends. There are many types available on amazon and local markets too. You can get a simple straight glass rod or one with a spiraling stem. Everything works. Make sure it reaches the bottom of your stirring glass while holding it comfortably high above the brim of the Mocktail mixture.

In this book, quite a few recipes will ask you go do something along the lines of "stir with ice and strain." In these recipes, follow the following steps:

- Pour accurate measurements of the ingredients into the stirring glass and put in ice until the stirring class is around 60-70% full.
- Stir the mixture rapidly for about 45 seconds. Make sure the bar spoon is close to the bottom and inner of the stirring glass as you stir.
- Pour the mixture into a serving glass through a strain, making sure the ice is left behind in the strain. If the drink is to be served with ice, place fresh ice in the serving glass first, then strain the mixture over it. Never use left over ice from the stirring glass, as it is almost always on the verge of melting.
- Discard the ice and clean the stirring glass before making the next batch.

# Muddling

A muddler is nothing more than a bartender's pestle. Muddling means smashing solid ingredients so that they go with the mocktail. Make sure you don't muddle in a glass vessel, as glass might crumble

# Measuring

Measurements are important. An approximation is fine; you will still need to be close to what the recipes ask for. Make sure you have a measuring device in your possession.

# Measurement Conversions

| STANDARD -> METRIC CONVERSIONS | | | | | |
|---|---|---|---|---|---|
| STANDARD MEASURE | | EQUIVALENT TO | | PRECISE CONVERSION | | APPROXIMATE CONVERSION |
| 1 tbsp | = | 3 tsp | = | 14.78677 mL | ≈ | 15 mL |
| 1 fl oz | = | 2 tbsp | = | 29.57353 mL | ≈ | 30 mL |
| 1 cup | = | 8 fl oz | = | 236.58824 mL | ≈ | 237 mL |
| 1 pint | = | 2 cups | = | 473.17648 mL | ≈ | 473 mL |
| 1 pint | = | 16 fl oz | = | 473.17648 mL | ≈ | 473 mL |
| 1 quart | = | 2 pints | = | 946.35296 mL | ≈ | 946 mL |
| 1 gallon | = | 4 quarts | = | 3.7854 L | ≈ | 3.8 L |
| 1 gallon | = | 128 fl oz | = | 3.7854 L | ≈ | 3.8 L |
| **1 gallon = 4 quarts = 8 pints = 16 cups = 128 fl oz** | | | | | | |
| www.math-salamanders.com | | | | | | |

# Chapter 4: Old-Fashioned and Classic Recipes

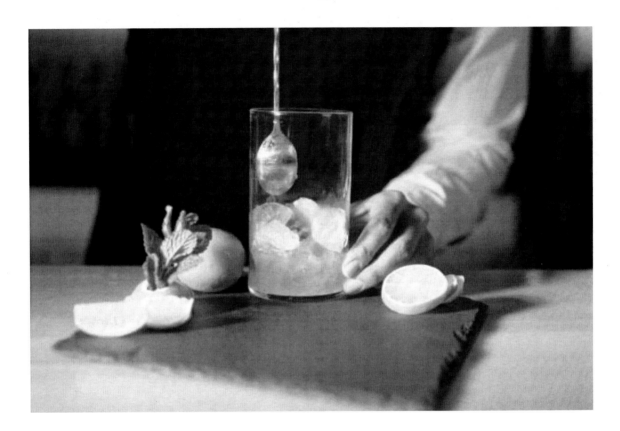

## 1.    Maple Mocktail

**Preparation Time:** 20 minutes

**Servings:** 4

**Ingredients:**

- 2 oz. Cranberry juice
- 2 oz. Apple juice
- 2 oz. Sparkling water
- 1 oz. Lemon juice
- 2 oz. Maple syrup
- Maple sugar and cinnamon stick to garnish

**Directions:**

- In a shaker, mix the first five ingredients and shake gently.
- Dim the rim of a footed pilsner glass with maple sugar.
- Strain the drink into the glass with ice.
- Garnish with a cinnamon stick.
- Enjoy!

## 2.    Mojito Mocktail

**Preparation Time:** 20 minutes

**Servings:** 4

**Ingredients:**

- Ice
- ½ oz. Lime juice
- 1 ½ oz. Mint simple syrup
- 3 oz. Club soda
- Lime slices and mint sprigs for garnish

**Directions:**

- Fill a tall glass with ice.
- Add the syrup, lime juice, and club soda.
- Stir until well-combined.
- Garnish with additional limes and mint
- Enjoy!

# 3.   Grapefruit & Tonic Mocktail

**Preparation Time:** 10 minutes

**Servings:** 2

**Ingredients:**

- 7-10 fresh blueberries
- 1-2 star anise
- 1 cucumber
- ½ grapefruit
- 6 oz. Tonic water
- 1 rosemary sprig

**Directions:**

- In a wine glass, combine the blueberries and the star anise.
- Peel and add three large sections of the cucumber.
- Peel a large section of the grapefruit and twist the rind into
- The glass rubs the peel on the inside and adds to the glass.
- Fill the glass with ice and add top it with quality tonic water
- Garnish the rosemary sprig and stir the drink well, using the sprig to maximize the aromatics.
- Enjoy!

# 4. Bloody Mary Mocktail

**Preparation Time:** 15 minutes

**Servings:** 3

**Ingredients:**

- 1 c. beet juice
- 1 lemon, juiced
- 3 tbsp. Simple syrup
- 2 c. sparkling water
- ¼ c. olive juice
- ¼ tsp hot sauce
- Ice cubes

**Directions:**

- Pour ingredients into a pitcher & mix well.
- Serve immediately in serving glasses.

# 5. Blueberry Mint Mocktail

**Preparation Time:** 60 minutes

**Servings:** 6

**Ingredients:**

- ½ c. blueberries
- ¼ c. honey
- ¼ c. fresh mint leaves
- 1 lemon, juiced
- 2 c. sparkling water
- ½ c. water
- Ice cubes for serving

**Directions:**

- In a pitcher, muddle the blueberries, honey, and mint leaves.
- Mix in lemon juice, sparkling water, and water. Chill the drink for 2 hours.
- Serve the drink in glasses with ice cubes.

# 6.　Hibiscus Sparkling Mocktail

**Preparation Time:** 50 minutes

**Servings:** 3

**Ingredients:**

- 4 c. boiling water
- 8 bags of hibiscus tea bags
- ½ c. maple syrup
- Ice cubes
- 2 c. sparkling water
- ¼ c. mint leaves
- Dried hibiscus leaves to garnish

**Directions:**

- Pour the boiling water into a pitcher and steep the tea bags for 2 to 3 minutes. Remove the tea bags after.
- Mix in the maple syrup and chill in the refrigerator for 2 hours.

- Take out the pitcher and mix in the sparkling water and mint leaves.
- Spoon the ice cubes into serving glasses and top them with the drink.
- Garnish with the hibiscus leaves and serve immediately.

# 7.    Hot and Cold Paloma Mocktail

**Preparation Time:** 15 minutes

**Servings:** 3

**Ingredients:**

- ½ peeled grapefruit
- 3 tbsp. Freshly squeezed lime juice
- 1 long red chili
- 2 tbsp. Simple syrup
- 3 c. sparkling water
- 2 fresh rosemary sprigs

**Directions:**

- Add ingredients to a pitcher, mix and chill in the refrigerator for 2 hours.
- Pour the drink into serving glasses.
- Serve immediately.

# 8.    Mock Champagne

**Preparation Time:** 10 minutes

**Servings:** 3

**Ingredients:**

- 2 c. ginger ale, chilled
- 1 c. pineapple juice, chilled
- 1 c. white grape juice, chilled
- Ice cubes for serving
- Raspberries to garnish

**Directions:**

- Mix ingredients in a pitcher & pour over ice cubes in serving glasses.
- Garnish with two raspberries each per glass and enjoy immediately!

# 9.    Orange Lavender Mocktail

**Preparation Time:** 10 minutes

**Servings:** 2

**Ingredients:**

- Ice
- 1 oz. Lavender syrup
- ½ c. orange juice
- ½ oz. Grenadine
- Orange wheel and lavender spring for garnish

**Directions:**

- Put the ice into a shaker.
- Add the lavender syrup.
- Add the orange juice.
- Add the grenadine.
- Shake well for 5-10 seconds.

- Pour it into a cold glass.

- Garnish with orange wheel and lavender spring.

- Enjoy!

# 10. Peach Mocktail

**Preparation Time:** 10 minutes

**Servings:** 2

**Ingredients:**

- 1 ripe peach already cut into slices and frozen

- 1 oz. Sugar

- ½ oz. Lime juice

- ½ c. apple juice

- Ice

- ½ c. sparkling water

- 2-4 leaves of fresh mint

**Directions:**

- Put the peach, sugar, lime juice, and apple juice in a blender.

- Blend until the mixture is smooth.

- Put ice cubes into a glass.

- Add mint and pour the mixture.

- Add mint leaves.

- Top with sparkling water and stir well.

- Enjoy!

# 11. Pear Rosemary Mocktail

**Preparation Time:** 45 minutes

**Servings:** 8

**Ingredients:**

- 1 lemon, juiced

- ½ c. pear juice
- 2 tbsp. Simple syrup
- 2 fresh rosemary sprigs
- 1 bottle of ginger beer

**Directions:**

- Mix ingredients in a pitcher & chill for 1 hour.
- Pour the drink into serving glasses and enjoy.

# 12.   Raspberry Passion Mocktail

**Preparation Time:** 10 minutes

**Servings:** 2

**Ingredients:**

- 1oz. Red grapefruit juice
- 2 oz. Raspberry syrup
- 1 c. soda water
- Ice
- 5-7 raspberries
- 1 rosemary spring

**Directions:**

- Put the ice in a shaker.
- Add the grapefruit juice and the raspberry syrup.
- Shake it.
- Put ice in the glass and pour the mixture.
- Top with soda water.
- Add fresh raspberries and garnish with a rosemary spring.
- Enjoy!

# 13. Rhubarb Ginger Mocktail

**Preparation Time:** 10 minutes

**Servings:** 2

**Ingredients:**

- Ice
- 2 oz. Rhubarb syrup
- 1 c. club soda
- 2 basil leaves
- 1 basil leaf and rosemary spring for garnish.

**Directions:**

- Add ice, syrup, club soda, and basil to a shaker.
- Stir it.
- Strain the Mocktail into a martini glass.
- Garnish with a basil leave and rosemary spring.
- Enjoy!

# 14. Rosemary Rhubarb Mocktail

**Preparation Time:** 15 minutes

**Servings:** 3

**Ingredients:**

- 2 oz. Club soda

- 1 oz. Rhubarb rosemary simple syrup

- Rosemary spring for garnish

- Ice

**Directions:**

- Pour the rhubarb syrup into a tall and thin glass.

- Top with club soda.

- Add large ice.

- Garnish with the rosemary spring.

- Enjoy!

# 15.  Sherbet Raspberry Mocktail

**Preparation Time:** 10 minutes

**Servings:** 3

**Ingredients:**

- 2 c. sprite

- 2 c. soda water

- 1 12 oz. can of pink lemonade

- ½ c. pineapple wedges

- ½ c. raspberries

- 8 scoops of raspberry sherbet ice cream, frozen

**Directions:**

- Mix the sprite, soda water, lemonade, pineapple wedges, and raspberries in a large glass bowl.
- Pour the drink into serving glasses and scoop one dollop of the ice cream onto each glass.
- Enjoy immediately!

# 16.    Thyme Mocktail

**Preparation Time:** 15 minutes

**Servings:** 3

**Ingredients:**

- 1 oz. Simple syrup
- 5 springs of fresh thyme
- 1 c. sparkling water
- ½ c. grapefruit juice
- Ice
- 1 spring of thyme for garnish

**Directions:**

- Put the fresh thyme into a shaker and syrup.
- Muddle the thyme.
- Add the grapefruit juice.
- Shake well for 5-10 seconds.
- Put ice into a glass.
- Strain the thyme mixture.
- Top with sparkling water.
- Garnish with a thyme spring.
- Enjoy!

# 17.    Watermelon Mocktail

**Preparation Time:** 15 minutes

**Servings:** 3

**Ingredients:**

- 60gr watermelon wedges/slice
- 1 oz. Strawberry syrup
- 5 oz. Soda water
- Ice
- Lime slice for garnish

**Directions:**

- Put watermelon wedges/slices into the glass, then muddle well.
- Add the strawberry syrup and 2 oz. Soda water.
- Stir well.
- Add ice and fill up with the remaining soda
- Garnish with a lime slice.
- Enjoy!

# 18.  Watermelon Mojito

**Preparation Time:** 15 minutes

**Servings:** 3

**Ingredients:**

- Sugar to rim the glass

- 2 small lime slices

- ½ oz. Lime juice

- 1 small bunch of fresh mint

- 1 ½ oz. Simple syrup

- ½ c. watermelon, blended

- Soda water

- Ice cubes

**Directions:**

- Put the watermelon into a blender and mix it until smooth.

- In a glass rimmed with sugar, put a slice of lime, mint leaves

- And lime juice. Muddle to take out the flavors.

- Add the syrup and the blended watermelon. Stir well.

- Top with soda water and add ice cubes

- Garnish with a spring of mint and lime wheel

- Enjoy!

# 19.   Lavender Mocktail

**Preparation Time:** 10 minutes

**Servings:** 3

**Ingredients:**

- 3 tsp fresh culinary lavender

- 2 tbsp. Honey

- 2 tbsp. Sugar

- 2 c. lemon juice

- 2 c. sparkling water

- Ice cubes for serving

**Directions:**

- Pour the lavender into a pitcher and muddle to crush the leaves a little.

- Add the remaining ingredients to the pitcher and mix well. Chill in the refrigerator for 1 hour.
- Pour the drink into serving glasses and serve with ice cubes if preferred.

# Chapter 5: Brunch Recipes

## 20.   Mint Julep

**Preparation Time:** 10 minutes

**Servings:** 3

**Ingredients:**

- 2 c. water (chilled)
- ¾ c. fresh lemon juice
- 1½ c. granulated sugar
- 6 fresh mint sprigs
- 5 c. ice
- 2½ c. ginger ale (chilled)
- Lemon slices (to garnish)

**Directions:**

- Stir the chilled water, lemon juice, sugar, and mint sprigs in a large bowl. Allow standing for 45 minutes to steep.
- Strain the mixture into a pitcher, and discard mint sprigs.
- Add ice to the pitcher and top up with chilled ginger ale. Garnish with lemon slices and serve!

# 21. Mock Mai Tai

**Preparation Time:** 10 minutes

**Servings:** 3

**Ingredients:**

- Ice
- ¼ c. fresh pineapple juice
- ½ c. fresh orange juice
- ½ c. lemon and lime soda
- 1 tbsp grenadine
- Maraschino cherry (to garnish)
- 1 orange slice (to garnish)

**Directions:**

- Fill a Mocktail glass halfway full with ice.
- Pour in the pineapple juice, orange juice, lemon and lime soda, and grenadine. Stir to combine.
- Garnish with a maraschino cherry and an orange slice.
- Serve straight away with a straw.

# 22. Passion Fruit Martini

**Preparation Time:** 10 minutes

**Servings:** 3

**Ingredients:**

- 3 passion fruits (cut in half)
- White of 1 medium egg
- Juice of 1 lemon

- ½ c. alcohol-free spirit of choice
- 2½ tsp sugar syrup
- Ice cubes
- Sparkling grape juice (chilled to top)

**Directions:**

- Scoop the pulp from 4 of the passion fruit halves into a Mocktail shaker. Add the egg white, lemon juice, alcohol-free spirit, and sugar syrup. Shake for 20-30 seconds until combined and frothy.
- Add ice to the Mocktail shaker and shake for another 20-30 seconds until the mixture is well chilled.
- Strain into two martini glasses and top up with sparkling grape juice.
- Float a passion half on top of each drink to garnish.

# 23.   Pomegranate Negroni

**Preparation Time:** 10 minutes

**Servings:** 3

**Ingredients:**

- 6¾ oz. pomegranate juice
- 2 tsp sugar-free cherry concentrate (chilled)
- Ice cubes

- 2-3 dashes of Angostura bitters
- Twist of orange peel

**Directions:**

- Add the pomegranate juice and cherry concentrate to an ice-filled rocks glass. Stir well to combine.
- Stir in the bitters to taste.
- Carefully twist the orange peel over the top to release its oils.
- Enjoy.

# 24.    Strawberry Daiquiri Mocktail

**Preparation Time:** 10 minutes

**Servings:** 2

**Ingredients:**

- 16 oz. strawberries (hulled)
- 7 oz. ice
- ½ c. lemonade
- Freshly squeezed juice of ½ lime
- 1 fresh strawberry (hulled and halved to garnish)
- 2 slices of fresh lime

**Directions:**

- Add the strawberries to a food blender and process until smooth.
- Push the puree through a mesh sieve to remove some of its seeds.
- Tip the now-sieved puree into the food blender and process once again.
- Divide the mixture between 2 margarita or martini glasses.
- Garnish with a fresh strawberry and a slice of lime.
- Serve.

# 25.   Mandarin Mojito Mocktail

**Preparation Time:** 5 minutes

**Servings:** 3

**Ingredients:**

- 8 fluid oz. sprite or 7up
- ½ of a fluid oz. Mandarin syrup
- ½ of a fluid oz. mojito mix
- 5 mandarin orange segments
- 3-5 large mint leaves
- 1 lime
- Mandarin orange segments as garnish

**Directions:**

- Cut the lime into at least two wedges.
- Place the two lime wedges, mint leaves & orange segments into your glass.
- Muddle the ingredients.
- Now place the rest of the ingredients into the glass.
- Stir the drink mixture.
- Add the desired amount of ice.

- Use additional orange segments for garnish.

# 26.   Sweet Virgin Sunrise

**Preparation Time:** 10 minutes

**Servings:** 4

**Ingredients:**

- 4 oz. orange juice, fresh-squeezed if possible
- Ice
- ½ oz. grenadine
- Orange slice for garnish

**Directions:**

- Pour ice into a highball glass and add the orange juice.
- Pour grenadine slowly over the juice.
- Use an orange slice to garnish and serve.

# 27.   The Classy Lady

**Preparation Time:** 10 minutes

**Servings:** 2

**Ingredients:**

- ¼ tsp salt
- 1 oz. sugar syrup
- 1 cucumber slice
- Ice
- 1 oz. fresh lime juice
- 2 oz. cranberry juice (chilled)

**Directions:**

- Add the salt, sugar syrup, and cucumber to a Mocktail shaker, use a muddler to 'smash,' and combine the ingredients.

- Add the ice to the shaker along with the lime and cranberry juice. Shake for 20-30 seconds until well chilled.
- Strain into a martini glass and enjoy!

# 28. Tropical Fruits

**Preparation Time:** 10 minutes

**Servings:** 4

**Ingredients:**

- 1 ¼ c. chopped strawberries
- 2 c. sparkling water
- 2 oranges juice

**Directions:**

- In a pitcher, add the strawberries and use a muddler to mash the fruits.
- Pour in the sparkling water and orange juice and cover the pitcher with plastic wrap.
- Chill in the refrigerator for 2 hours.
- Serve the drink in glasses.

# 29. Tuscan Fresco

**Preparation Time:** 10 minutes

**Servings:** 1

**Ingredients:**

- Ice made with filtered water
- 2 sprigs rosemary
- 1 oz. peach nectar
- 1 oz. White cranberry juice
- ½ oz. Fresh orange juice
- ½ oz. store-bought simple syrup
- 1 oz. Chilled club soda

**Directions:**

- Add ice to Mocktail shaker till full.
- Add a sprig of rosemary and the simple syrup, orange juice, cranberry juice, and peach nectar.
- Shake to combine thoroughly. Strain into ice-filled glass.
- Stir club soda. Use the remaining sprig of rosemary to garnish. Serve.

# 30. Virgin Bloody Mary with Shrimp

**Preparation Time:** 5 minutes

**Servings:** 3

**Ingredients:**

- 22 oz. reduced-sodium v8
- 1 tsp. horseradish
- 1 tsp. Worcestershire sauce
- 1 tbsp. lemon juice
- 10 dashes tabasco
- Freshly ground pepper, to taste
- Ice cubes
- 4 cooked shrimp

**Directions:**

- Combine the v8, Worcestershire sauce, horseradish, tabasco, lemon juice & pepper in a glass jar.

- Apply to lid and shake.

- Place ice into two tall glasses.

- Evenly divide the drink mixture between the two glasses.

- Use the two shrimp as garnish.

# 31.   Virgin Pimm's

**Preparation Time:** 10 minutes

**Servings:** 2

**Ingredients:**

For the Red Infusion:

- 1 tsp allspice berries

- 2 tbsp juniper berries

- 1 tsp coriander seeds

- 1 tsp anise seeds

- 2 c. alcohol-free red wine

- Zest of 1 grapefruit

For the White Infusion:

- 2 tbsp juniper berries

- 1 tsp coriander seeds

- 1 tsp anise seeds
- 2 c. alcohol-free white wine
- Zest of 1 lemon

For the Pimm's:

- 3 tbsp fresh lemon juice
- 6 black tea bags
- 3 tsp fresh ginger (grated)
- 3 tsp brown sugar
- Ice cubes
- 12 oz. ginger beer
- Cucumber (very thinly sliced to garnish)

**Directions:**

- First, make the red infusion. Add the allspice, juniper berries, coriander seeds, and anise seeds to a small pan over moderate heat. Toast for 3 minutes. Transfer to a bowl.
- Add the wine and grapefruit zest to the spices. Stir and cover with plastic wrap. Allow steeping for 3 hours.
- In the meantime, prepare the white infusion. Toast the berries and seeds as before, then add to a bowl along with the wine and lemon zest. Stir to combine and allow to steep for 3 hours.
- Strain both infusions into separate resealable jars*.
- For each serving, add 5 tbsp. Red infusion and 3 tbsp white infusion to a Mocktail shaker along with ½ tbsp lemon juice, one tea bag, ½ tsp grated ginger, and ½ tsp brown sugar. Muddle the mixture. Set aside to steep for 5 minutes.
- Fill a tall glass halfway full with ice. Strain the liquid into the glass and top up with 2 ounces of ginger beer. Stir gently using a straw or metal stirrer. Garnish with a cucumber slice and serve straight away.

*Infusions will keep for up to 30 days chilled.

# 32.   Zesty Ginger Strawberry Cooler

**Preparation Time:** 10 minutes

**Servings:** 2

**Ingredients:**

- ½ oz. sugar syrup
- ½" chunk of fresh ginger (peeled, grated)
- 2-3 fresh strawberries (hulled, sliced)
- Ice cubes
- 1 oz. fresh lime juice
- 2 oz. fresh orange juice
- 2 oz. ginger beer (chilled)

**Directions:**

- Add the sugar syrup, ginger, and strawberries to a Mocktail shaker, use a muddler to 'smash,' and combine the ingredients.
- Add the ice to the shaker, lime juice, and orange juice. Shake for 20-30 seconds until well chilled and combined.
- Strain the liquid into a glass filled with more ice.
- Top up with chilled ginger beer.
- Serve straight away.

# 33.   Strawberry Basil Soda

**Preparation Time:** 5 minutes

**Servings:** 3

**Ingredients:**

- 1 lb. of strawberries, trimmed
- The juice of half a lemon
- ½ of a c. loosely packed basil leaves
- 1 c. sugar
- Carbonated water

**Directions:**

- Using your knife & cutting board, trim the strawberries.
- Place the berries into your blender and process until smooth.

- Transfer the berries to the sieve and push through using your spatula.
- Toss the solids and pour the juice into your measuring cup.
- Add sufficient water to fill-up the cup.
- Put the basil, lemon juice, and sugar into the saucepan.
- Place the pan over medium heat.
- Cook until boiling.
- Reduce the heat and allow the mixture to simmer for five minutes.
- Stir often while the mixture is cooking.
- Take the pan off of the heat and set it aside to cool.
- Pour the syrupy mixture through the sieve into your container.
- Toss solids.
- Now spoon two tablespoons of syrup into your glass.
- Pour carbonated water on top & stir.
- Serve and enjoy.

# Chapter 6: Lunch Recipes

## 34.   Arnold Palmer

**Preparation Time:** 10 minutes

**Servings:** 2

**Ingredients:**

- 2 parts of iced tea for each
- 1 part of lemonade for each

For garnishing:

- Slices of lemon

**Directions:**

- Pour iced tea and lemonade into two ice-filled tall glasses.
- Stir thoroughly.
- Garnish with lemon slices. Serve.

# 35.   Raspberry-Cranberry Twist

This mocktail is extremely easy to make and tastes delicious. It is a perfect holiday non-alcoholic drink.

**Preparation Time:** 2 minutes

**Servings:** 2

**Ingredients:**

- 1 x 12 fluid oz. Bottle or can of carbonated beverage (lemon-lime flavor)
- 12 fluid oz. cranberry-raspberry juice

**Directions:**

- Mix the lemon-lime soda with cranberry-raspberry juice. Pour it over ice. Serve.

# 36.   No-Wine Baby Bellini

**Preparation Time:** 10 minutes

**Servings:** 2

**Ingredients:**

- 2 fluid oz. cider (sparkling)
- 2 fluid oz. peach nectar
- 1 peach slice for garnishing optional

**Directions:**

- Pour peach nectar into a champagne flute.
- Add sparkling cider slowly.
- Use a peach slice to garnish, if desired. Serve.

# 37.   Berry Shrub Mocktail

**Preparation Time:** 10 minutes

**Servings:** 2

**Ingredients:**

- 2 c. rinsed, drained, crushed blackberries (2 c., fresh, rinsed)
- 2 c. sugar, white

Optional:

- 2 thyme sprigs
- 2 sage sprigs
- 1 c. vinegar, white

**Directions:**

- Wash, then sterilize a jar or bowl.
- Add the blackberries and cover them with white sugar. Add sage and thyme.
- Combine by stirring.
- Cover jar or bowl with cling wrap or lid. Place in refrigerator and occasionally stir for one to two days, till you have a pool of syrup and juice formed around berries.
- Remove sage and thyme sprigs.
- Place a fine strainer over a separate bowl. Pour the blackberry mixture in. Press on solids lightly so all juice is expelled.
- Sterilize a bottle or glass jar. Add juice and vinegar. Cover and gently shake to help the sugar dissolve fully.
- Allow to rest till the flavors have intensified – one day or longer. Serve.

# 38.  Agave Grapefruit Mocktail

**Preparation Time:** 20 minutes

**Servings:** 4

**Ingredients:**

- 2 oz. Grapefruit juice
- ½ oz. Lime juice
- ¼ oz. Agave nectar
- Pinch of cinnamon
- 1 bottle (100 ml) of bitter red soda
- Sprig of rosemary for garnish

**Directions:**

- Into a shaking tin, combine de grapefruit juice, lime juice, and agave nectar.
- Add a pinch of ground cinnamon.
- Shake it up.
- Pour it into a Collins glass with ice.
- Mix it with 3 oz. bitter red soda.
- Garnish with a spring of rosemary.
- Enjoy!

# 39.  Chamomile Mocktail

**Preparation Time:** 20 minutes

**Servings:** 4

**Ingredients:**

- 8 mint leaves
- 1 oz. Chamomile simple syrup
- 1oz. Ginger simple syrup
- 1/4 c. cranberry juice
- 1 bottle of ginger beer

**Directions:**

- Put the mint leaves into a shaker.
- Add the chamomile syrup, ginger syrup, and muddle.
- Add cranberry juice and ice.
- Shake well.
- Strain into a glass
- Top with ginger beer
- Enjoy!

# 40.   Cherry Lime Mocktail

**Preparation Time:** 10 minutes

**Servings:** 2

**Ingredients:**

- 1 c. soda water
- 1 ½ oz. Cherry syrup
- 1 ½ lime juice
- 4-5 fresh cherries
- Mint spring for garnish

**Directions:**

- Put ice on a tall glass.
- Add the sherry syrup and lime juice.
- Top it with soda water and stir.
- And the fresh cherries and garnish with the mint spring.
- Enjoy!

# 41.   Cucumber Lemon Punch

**Preparation Time:** 10 minutes

**Servings:** 2

**Ingredients:**

- 12 fluid oz. grape juice concentrate (white, canned)
- 1 x .14-oz. package of lemonade powder (instant, sugar-free)
- 3 quarts of cubed ice
- 3 quarts of water (filtered)
- ½ sliced cucumber, medium
- 1 sliced lemon

**Directions:**

- Stir water, grape juice concentrate, powdered lemonade, and cubed ice in a punch bowl.
- Slice cucumbers and lemon and set slices floating on top of the liquid.
- Serve.

# 42. Elderflower Mocktail

**Preparation Time:** 20 minutes

**Servings:** 4

**Ingredients:**

- 1 oz. Raspberry syrup
- ¼ oz. Lemon juice
- 2 oz. Elderflower tea
- Soda water
- Ice cubes
- 5 fresh raspberries
- Mint spring for garnish

**Directions:**

- Pour raspberry syrup, lime juice, and tea into the glass
- Add ice cubes
- Fill up with soda water
- Add the fresh raspberries and garnish with mint

- Enjoy!

# 43.   Ginger Lime Mule

**Preparation Time:** 10 minutes

**Servings:** 2

**Ingredients:**

- 1½ oz. Ginger-lime syrup
- 6 oz. Soda water
- Candied ginger for garnish

**Directions:**

- In a shaker, combine the ginger-lime syrup and soda water.
- Stir gently, then double strain it over ice in a Collins glass.
- Garnish with a piece of candied ginger.
- Enjoy!

# 44.   Lime Pom Pom

**Preparation Time:** 10 minutes

**Servings:** 2

**Ingredients:**

- Ice made from filtered water
- ½ oz. Mango juice or nectar
- 1 oz. Pomegranate juice
- ½ oz. Lime juice, fresh
- ½ oz. Tea
- 1 oz. Club soda, chilled
- 1 orange fruit wheel (sliced from the mid-section of an orange)

**Directions:**

- Fill the Mocktail shaker with ice.
- Add lime juice, tea, mango juice, and pomegranate juice. Shake and combine.
- Strain into a pre-chilled martini glass. Then top with club soda. Use an orange wheel for garnishing. Serve.

# 45. Not a Hot Toddy

**Preparation Time:** 10 minutes

**Servings:** 2

**Ingredients:**

- 1 tbsp. Organic Honey
- 1 tsp. Lemon juice, fresh
- ½ tsp. Ground nutmeg
- ½ tsp. Cloves
- ½ tsp. Cinnamon, grated
- 7 fluid oz. Hot tea

For Garnishing:

- Wedge of lemon

**Directions:**

- Add honey, lemon juice, and spices to a warm mug.

- Top with fresh-brewed, hot tea. Stir well to combine.
- Use a lemon wedge to garnish and serve.

# 46.  Orange Rose Mocktail

**Preparation Time:** 20 minutes

**Servings:** 4

**Ingredients:**

- 1 oz. Orange syrup
- 1 oz. Rose syrup
- 1 oz. Lime juice
- Ginger ale
- Ice cubes
- Orange wheel for garnish

**Directions:**

- Pour orange syrup and lime juice into the glass.
- Add ice cubes and then pour rose syrup.
- Fill up with ginger ale.
- Garnish with an orange wheel.
- Enjoy!

# 47.  Peach Sunrise

**Preparation Time:** 10 minutes

**Servings:** 2

**Ingredients:**

- 3 fluid oz. peach juice (fresh)
- 4 fluid oz. 7-up or other lemon-lime flavored soda
- ¾ fluid oz. grenadine

**Directions:**

- Add ice to a highball glass.
- Pour in peach juice.
- Fill the glass with lemon-lime soda.
- Pour grenadine slowly into the drink. It sinks and then gradually rises, mixing with the soda and juice. Serve.

# 48.  Roy Rogers

**Preparation Time:** 10 minutes

**Servings:** 2

**Ingredients:**

- ¼ oz. grenadine
- 8 oz. cola-flavored soda
- 1 maraschino cherry for garnishing

**Directions:**

- Fill a tall glass with ice. Pour in grenadine.
- Add cola and stir to combine.
- Use maraschino cherry for garnishing and serve.

# 49.  Tuscan Fresco

**Preparation Time:** 10 minutes

**Servings:** 2

**Ingredients:**

- Ice made with filtered water
- 2 sprigs of rosemary
- 1 fluid oz. peach nectar
- 1 fluid oz. cranberry juice (white)
- ½ fluid oz. lemon juice (fresh)
- ½ fluid oz. simple syrup (store-bought)
- 1 fluid oz. Club soda (chilled)

**Directions:**

- Add ice to the Mocktail shaker till full.
- Add a sprig of rosemary and the simple syrup, lemon juice, cranberry juice, and peach nectar.
- Shake to combine thoroughly. Strain into ice-filled glass.
- Stir club soda. Use the remaining sprig of rosemary to garnish. Serve.

# 50.   Virgin Appletini

**Preparation Time:** 10 minutes

**Servings:** 2

**Ingredients:**

- ¼ fluid oz. lemon juice (fresh if available)
- ½ fluid oz. simple syrup (pre-bottled)
- 2 fluid oz. apple juice

For Dipping Rim:

- Sugar, white

For Garnishing:

- 1 slice of apple

**Directions:**

- Fill the Mocktail shaker with ice.
- Pour lemon juice, syrup, and apple juice into a shaker and shake it well.
- Strain into a sugar-rimmed glass.
- Garnish with a slice of apple and serve.

# Chapter 7: Dinner Recipes

## 51.  Berry Mocktail

**Preparation Time:** 10 minutes

**Servings:** 2

**Ingredients:**

- 1 32 oz. bottle cranberry juice Mocktail, chilled
- 1 container of raspberry sherbet
- ½ liter lemon soda, chilled

**Directions:**

- Pour ¼ cup of chilled cranberry juice into short glasses. Add one scoop of raspberry sherbet and top with lemon soda.
- Serve.

# 52. Ginger-Blueberry Mocktail

**Preparation Time:** 10 minutes

**Servings:** 2

**Ingredients:**

- 3 ½ c. water
- 1 tbsp. Freshly grated ginger
- 1 ½ c. fresh blueberries
- 5 tbsp. Sugar
- 2 c. sparkling water
- Ice cubes for serving
- Thin orange and lemon zest to garnish

**Directions:**

- In a med pan, mix the water, ginger, and blueberries. Allow boiling with frequent stirring until the sugar dissolves.
- Reduce the heat to low; use a spatula to break the blueberries until mashed and mix in the sugar. Turn the heat off, cover the pot with plastic wrap, and allow cooling for 2 to 3 hours in the refrigerator. This process infuses the flavors.
- Strain the mixture into a serving glass jar and top it with sparkling water and ice cubes.
- Stir and pour the drink into serving glasses, garnish with the orange and lemon zest, and serve warm.

# 53. Bloody Mary

**Preparation Time:** 10 minutes

**Servings:** 2

**Ingredients:**

- Tomato juice
- 3 dashes of Worcestershire sauce
- Celery salt

- Tabasco sauce (optional)
- Lime for garnish
- Ice cubes or cracked ice

**Directions:**

- Fill a highball glass or tumbler with ice cubes or cracked ice.
- Fill to the top with your choice of tomato juice.
- Add three dashes of Worcestershire sauce and a sprinkle of celery seed and stir.
- Serve with a slice of lime for garnish.
- Squeeze the lime into the drink before drinking for more flavor.
- For a spicy version of this drink, add a few dashes of tabasco sauce.

# 54. Cranberry Lemonade Mocktail

**Preparation Time:** 10 minutes

**Servings:** 2

**Ingredients:**

- 2 c. cranberry juice, chilled
- 2 c. berry sparkling water, chilled
- 6 oz. Pink lemonade concentrate, chilled
- Crushed ice

- Cranberries for topping
- 1 lemon, thinly sliced to garnish

**Directions:**

- Combine the cranberry juice, sparkling water, and lemonade concentrate in a pitcher.
- Pour ice into serving glasses and top with the drink.
- Top with the cranberries, garnish with the lemon wedges and serve immediately.

# 55. Crimson Poison

**Preparation Time:** 10 minutes

**Servings:** 2

**Ingredients:**

- Colored sugar
- 1 slice lime
- ½ c. strawberries
- 1 tbsp. lingonberry syrup (can be replaced with other sweeteners or berry-based syrup)
- 1 tsp. fresh lime juice
- Ice
- Tonic water

**Directions:**

- On a saucer, pour the sugar and spread it around.
- Pass the slice of lime on the rim of the glass to wet it, then turn it upside down on the saucer to cover the rim with sugar. Set aside.
- In a blender, place the strawberries, lingonberry syrup, lime juice, and ice. Pulse until the mixture becomes smooth.
- Pour the mixture into the glass, and then add the tonic water until full. Stir.
- Garnish with a slice of lime and serve immediately.

# 56.  Dead Man's Finger Mocktails

**Preparation Time:** 10 minutes

**Servings:** 2

**Ingredients:**

- ½ c. Hawaiian punch
- ½ c. diet 7-up
- Vanilla ice cream about ¼ c. scoop
- Fake blood - light corn syrup dyed with red food coloring

**Directions:**

- Pour ½ cup Hawaiian punch into the bottom of the glass, then place a small scoop of vanilla ice cream in the glass
- Carefully pour about ½ cup of diet 7-up over the ice cream.
- Pop the severed finger ice cubes out of the tray and place them in the glass.

# 57.  Dragon's Blood Punch

**Preparation Time:** 10 minutes

**Servings:** 2

**Ingredients:**

- 1 (46 oz.) can of red punch (recommended: Hawaiian punch)
- 1 (46 oz.) can of apple juice
- 1 (48 oz.) bottle of cranberry juice
- 1 (2-litre) bottle of ginger ale
- Ice cubes
- Berry vodka, optional
- Orange liqueur, optional

**Directions:**

- Combine all ingredients in a large punch bowl or pot. Add ice and stir.
- Add 4 cups of berry vodka and ½ cup of orange liqueur for the grown-up version.
- Ladle into serving glasses.

# 58.   Lime Pineapple Mocktail

**Preparation Time:** 10 minutes

**Servings:** 2

**Ingredients:**

- Edible gold glitter
- Juice from 1 lime
- Ice (about a handful)
- 1 tsp. clear honey
- Coriander leaves (a small bunch)
- 750ml pineapple juice
- 400ml tonic water

**Directions:**

- Get honey and dip a pastry brush into it. On one side of 4 tumblers, use this to paint a line down.
- Drizzle edible gold glitter and get rid of the excess. Place the tumblers in the refrigerator

- Cut the coriander leaves into small pieces and transfer them into a Mocktail shaker. Add ice, 100ml pineapple juice, and lime juice, and shake the Mocktail shaker so that the outer part feels chill.
- Strain this mixture into the tumblers and top with more ice cubes. Distribute the tonic water and the rest of the pineapple juice among the glasses.

# 59.   Love Potion

**Preparation Time:** 10 minutes

**Servings:** 2

**Ingredients:**

- 1 c. strawberry crush
- 1 c. orange juice
- 2 tbsps. lemon juice
- 5 c. crushed ice
- 4 strawberries, sliced
- A few sprigs of fresh mint

**Directions:**

- Blend the strawberry crush, orange juice, lemon juice, and crushed ice well.
- Pour into individual glasses, decorate with strawberry slices and mint sprigs and serve.

# 60.  Madame Guillotine

**Preparation Time:** 10 minutes

**Servings:** 2

**Ingredients:**

- 1 c. watermelon puree
- 1 tsp. grenadine syrup
- Juice from 1 orange
- 1 tbsp. granulated sugar
- 2 c. ice cubes

**Directions:**

- Place all ingredients in a martini shaker and shake for 20 seconds.
- Strain the chilled liquid into a sugar-rimmed martini glass.

# 61.  Raspberry Virgin Mojito

**Preparation Time:** 10 minutes

**Servings:** 2

**Ingredients:**

- 15 mint leaves
- 2 tbsp. Simple syrup
- 1 lime, juiced
- 2 c. sparkling lemonade
- 1 c. raspberries + extra for garnishing

**Directions:**

- Mix the mint leaves, syrup, lime juice, lemonade, and raspberries in a pitcher.
- Cover with plastic wrap and chill in your refrigerator for 3 hours.
- Pour the drink halfway up the serving glasses and garnish with raspberries.
- Serve immediately.

# 62.   Red Devil

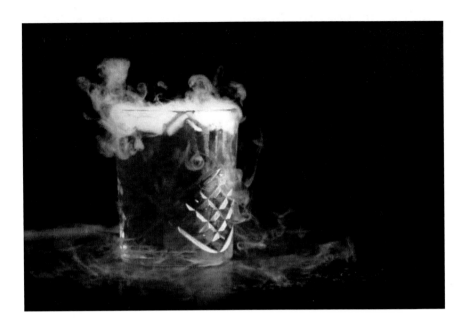

**Preparation Time:** 5 minutes

**Servings:** 1

**Ingredients:**

- 120ml water
- 30ml cranberry juice
- Twinings Blackcurrant & Blueberry Tea Bag
- 20ml Monin cassis
- Ice cubes

**Directions:**

- Tea bags should be steeped for 1-2 minutes in freshly boiled water.
- Add the syrup to an ice-filled glass or large jug.
- Add cranberry juice on top.
- Over the ice, pour the hot tea.
- A devil cocktail pick and some red berries can be added as a garnish after a thorough stirring.

# 63.   Rhubarb Cordial

**Preparation Time:** 10 minutes

**Servings:** 2

**Ingredients:**

- Juice and zest from 1 orange
- 450g of rhubarb (should be chopped)
- 300g of golden caster sugar
- Juice and zest from 1 lemon
- 1 fresh root ginger slice (should be peeled)

**Directions:**

- In a large saucepan, add about 300ml of water. Allow to come to a simmer, then include the juice and zest of the lemon and orange. Also, add the ginger and rhubarb
- Over medium heat, cook this combo so that the rhubarb crumbles
- Line a sieve with muslin and pour the mixture into a jug (heatproof). Pour the mixture in the jug into bottles, and you can store it in the refrigerator for up to 30 days

Per 100ml of sparkling water, you can serve about 25ml of cordial.

# 64.    Strawberry Orange Mocktail

**Preparation Time:** 10 minutes

**Servings:** 2

**Ingredients:**

- 1 ¼ c. strawberries, chopped
- 2 c. sparkling water
- 2 oranges, juiced

**Directions:**

- In a pitcher, add the strawberries and use a muddler to mash the fruits.
- Pour in the sparkling water and orange juice and cover the pitcher with plastic wrap. Chill in the refrigerator for 2 hours.
- Serve the drink in glasses.

# 65.   Summer Cup Mocktail

**Preparation Time:** 10 minutes

**Servings:** 2

**Ingredients:**

- 1 mint sprig
- 120 ml clear sparkling lemonade
- 1 cm thickness of cucumber slice
- Frozen red berries (about a small handful)
- Ice (about a handful)

For Garnish:

- Chopped fruits
- More frozen berries
- Citrus
- Mint
- Cucumber slice

**Directions:**

- Start by cutting the mint sprig and cucumber to form little pieces.

- In a small pan, add 200 ml of water and allow it to come to a boil. Include the chopped cucumber and mint pieces in the water. Put off the heat and allow to sit for about 2 minutes
- Include the frozen berries and leave them to thaw for about 1 minute. Use the back of a spoon to squash the berries, then strain the blend
- Store in the refrigerator for up to 24 hours. This can yield about four drinks
- In a tall glass, transfer about 40ml of the strained blend. Include the ice with the mixture and pour lemonade.
- Use any chopped fruit to garnish the drink, or you can use more mint leaves or frozen berries if available. Gently stir to mix the drink.

# 66.   Watermelon Agua Fresca

**Preparation Time:** 10 minutes

**Servings:** 2

**Ingredients:**

- 4 c. cubed watermelon
- 1 lime, juiced
- 3 c. water
- 2 tbsp. Sugar
- Watermelon wedges to garnish

**Directions:**

- Mix the watermelon, sugar, 1 cup of water, and lime juice in a blender.
- Strain the mixture through a colander into a pitcher and discard the solids.
- Mix in the remaining water and chill in the refrigerator for 2 hours.
- Pour the drink into halfway serving glasses and garnish with some watermelon wedges.
- Serve immediately.

# 67.   Blueberry Orange Ginger Mocktail

**Preparation Time:** 10 minutes

**Servings:** 2

**Ingredients:**

- 1 ¼ c. strawberries, chopped
- 2 c. sparkling water
- 2 oranges, juiced

**Directions:**

- In a pitcher, add the strawberries and use a muddler to mash the fruits.
- Pour in the sparkling water and orange juice and cover the pitcher with plastic wrap. Chill in the refrigerator for 2 hours.
- Serve the drink in glasses.

# 68.    Raspberry Orange Ginger Mocktail

**Preparation Time:** 10 minutes

**Servings:** 2

**Ingredients:**

- 2 ½ c. water
- 1 c. orange juice
- 1 tbsp. Freshly grated ginger
- 1 ½ c. fresh raspberries
- 5 tbsp. Sugar

- 2 c. sparkling water
- Ice cubes for serving
- Thin orange and lemon zest to garnish

**Directions:**

- In a med saucepan, combine the water, orange juice, ginger, and blueberries. Allow boiling with frequent stirring until the sugar dissolves.
- Reduce the heat to low; use a spatula to break the blueberries until mashed and mix in the sugar. Turn the heat off, cover the pot with plastic wrap, and allow cooling for 2 to 3 hours in the refrigerator. This process infuses the flavors.
- Strain into a serving glass jar and top with the sparkling water and ice cubes.
- Stir and pour the drink into serving glasses, garnish with the orange and lemon zest, and serve warm.

# 69. Grapefruit Thyme Mocktail

**Preparation Time:** 10 minutes

**Servings:** 2

**Ingredients:**

- ½ c. simple syrup
- ½ c. fresh thyme
- 4 c. sparkling water
- 1 ½ c. grapefruit juice
- 2 c. ice cubes

**Directions:**

- Mix up all the ingredients in a pitcher apart from the ice cubes. Cover with plastic wrap and chill in the refrigerator for 2 hours.
- Spoon some ice cubes into serving glasses and pour the drink on top. Garnish with the thyme sprigs & serve immediately.

# 70.  Rhubarb Citrus Mocktail

**Preparation Time:** 10 minutes

**Servings:** 6

**Ingredients:**

- 2 c. rhubarb juice
- 2 lemons, juiced
- ¼ c. simple syrup
- 1 ½ c. sparkling water
- Ice cubes for serving
- Mint leaves for garnishing
- Edible flowers for garnishing

**Directions:**

- Combine the rhubarb juice, lemon juice, syrup, and sparkling water in a pitcher. Chill for 2 hours.
- Spoon the ice cubes into serving glasses and pour the drink over them.
- Garnish with mint leaves and edible flowers. Serve immediately.

# Chapter 8: Dessert Recipes

## 71.  Shirley Ginger

**Preparation Time:** 10 minutes

**Servings:** 1

**Cooking Time:** 5 minutes

**Ingredients:**

- ½ tbsp. grenadine
- ⅓ c. lime-flavored soda
- ⅓ c. ginger ale
- Cherries to garnish
- Lime slices to garnish
- Ice cubes per requirement

**Directions:**

- Bring out your Mocktail shaker and pour in the ginger ale, lime soda, and grenadine.
- Fill ice into the shaker and start shaking it well.
- Pour the contents of the shaker into your serving glass along with the ice.
- Slice your lime into thin roundels. Garnish with the slices and top it off with sweet cherries. Serve chilled.

# 72.   Tahitian Coffee

**Preparation Time:** 10 minutes

**Servings:** 2

**Cooking Time:** 10 minutes

**Ingredients:**

- 2 oz. lime juice
- 2 oz. orange juice
- 1 oz. simple syrup
- 1 oz. passion fruit puree
- 2 oz. guava puree
- 2 oz. chilled concentrate coffee brew
- 3 oz. honey syrup
- Ice cubes as per requirement

**Directions:**

- For this mocktail, you could either use a blender or a Mocktail shaker for this recipe.
- Pour the lime juice and orange juice into your blender and give it a mix. Don't blend for long - just enough for the ingredients to mix.
- Now, add passion fruit puree and guava puree. Give it a blend and add the simple syrup and the honey syrup.
- Pour in the brewed coffee along with some ice. Blend it till all the liquids mix well.
- Add some ice to your serving glasses. Pour it equally into both glasses.

- Sprinkle a bit of coffee powder onto the top and garnish with thin guava slices and orchid flowers. Serve chilled.

# 73. Winter Shandy

**Preparation Time:** 10 minutes

**Servings:** 1

**Cooking Time:** 5 minutes

**Ingredients:**

- 2 oz. spice 94
- 1 oz. spiced apricot shrub
- 2 tsp. lemon juice
- 1 tsp. regular sugar or sugar syrup
- 3 oz. non-alcoholic beer
- Grapefruit zest to garnish
- Grated nutmeg to garnish
- Ice cubes as per requirement

**Directions:**

- Take out your Mocktail shaker and add the spice 94 to it.
- Pour the apricot shrub, sugar syrup, and lime juice.

- Fill the shaker with ice and begin shaking it to mix it well.
- Fill your serving glass with ice if needed. Pour the contents of the shaker into the glass.
- Pour in the non-alcoholic beer and stir the mix.
- Take a grapefruit and grate tout its zest. Do the same with the nutmeg.
- Sprinkle the grated nutmeg and the grapefruit zest over the mocktail and serve chilled.

# 74.  Cranberry Rose Fizz

**Preparation Time:** 10 minutes

**Servings:** 1

**Cooking Time:** 10 minutes

**Ingredients:**

- ¼ c. sugar
- ¼ c. water
- ⅛ tsp. cardamom
- 1 c. fresh cranberries
- 1 oz. rose water
- 4 oz. sparkling water or soda
- 3 oz. ginger ale
- Ice cubes as per requirement
- Cranberries to garnish

**Directions:**

- Bring out a saucepan and heat it over a medium-high flame. Add cranberries, cardamom, sugar, and water.
- Let the mixture boil, and then bring down the temperate to allow it to simmer for five minutes.
- The cranberries must pop and form a jam-like consistency. Take the pot out of the stove. Let it cool down for some time.
- Bring out your serving glass and add a tablespoon of cranberry jam. Store the rest.
- Filly the glass with ice to the level you prefer.
- Pour the rose water, sparkling water, soda, and ginger ale. Give the mocktail a good stir. Garnish with cranberries and serve chilled.

# 75.  Frozen Piña Coladas

**Preparation Time:** 5 minutes

**Servings:** 4

**Ingredients:**

- ¼ c. ice
- 1½ c. frozen pineapple chunks
- 1 c. unsweetened coconut milk
- 1 c. pineapple juice
- 1 tbsp brown sugar
- Maraschino cherries (to garnish)

**Directions:**

- Add the ice and frozen pineapple to a blender. Pour over the coconut milk and pineapple juice. Sweeten with brown sugar.
- Blitz until smooth and combined. Taste and add more sugar if needed.
- Pour into two tall Mocktail glasses and garnish each with a cherry.
- Serve straight away.

# 76.   Fun Faux Fizz

**Preparation Time:** 5 minutes

**Servings:** 5

**Ingredients:**

For the Syrup:

- 1 pear (cored and sliced)
- 4 dried apricots
- 2½ oz. golden caster sugar
- 1¼ tbsp runny honey
- Sprig of rosemary
- 1 lemon zest strip
- 3½ oz. water

For the Fizz:

- 2 tsp apple cider vinegar
- Sparkling mineral water
- A sprig of rosemary (to garnish)

**Directions:**

- For the syrup, add the pear slices, dried apricots, sugar, honey, a sprig of rosemary, and a lemon zest strip to a pan along with the water.
- Heat until the pear softens, and the sugar entirely dissolves for 10 minutes. Allow cooling completely.
- Strain the syrup through a fine-mesh strainer into a jug.
- Add the apple cider vinegar and place it in the refrigerator to chill for a minimum of 30 minutes.
- Pour approximately 1¾ tablespoons of the syrup into a champagne flute.
- Top with chilled sparkling mineral water.
- Garnish with a sprig of rosemary and serve.

# 77.  Gin-Free G&T

**Preparation Time:** 2 hours 10 minutes

**Servings:** 3

**Ingredients:**

- 5 cardamom pods
- ½ English cucumber (sliced)
- 1 chamomile tea bag
- 1 lemon zest strip
- ½ bunch of mint leaves
- ½ bunch rosemary
- 5 whole cloves
- Tonic water (as needed)
- Ice
- Pomegranate arils (to garnish)

**Directions:**

- Bruise the cardamom pods and add them along with the sliced cucumber to a large jug.
- Next, add the tea bag, followed by the lemon zest, mint leaves, cloves, rosemary, and cloves.
- Pour in 2 cups of cold water. Set aside to infuse in the refrigerator for 3 hours.

- To serve, strain the infused water into a measuring jug.
- Pour 1¾ ounces of the infused water into each glass.
- Fill with tonic water along with lots of ice.
- Garnish with mint leaves and pomegranate arils and serve.

# 78. Hibiscus Swizzle

**Preparation Time:** 10 minutes

**Servings:** 1

**Ingredients:**

For the Hibiscus Syrup:

- 8 oz. simple syrup (hot)
- 2 hibiscus flavor tea bags

For the Mocktail:

- ¾ oz. freshly squeezed lemon juice
- 3 oz. youngberry juice
- ¾ oz. hibiscus syrup
- 1 oz. Club soda (chilled)

**Directions:**

- For the hibiscus syrup: in a heat-safe bowl, combine the simple hot syrup with the tea bags and allow to infuse for 5 minutes,
- Remove and discard the tea bags and allow the syrup to cool.
- Transfer the mixture to a jar, cover it with a lid, and place it in the fridge for no more than 14 days. Use as directed.
- For the mocktail: add the fresh lemon juice, youngberry juice, and prepared hibiscus syrup to a Mocktail shaker filled with ice. Shake to combine.
- Strain the mixture into an ice-filled Collins glass.
- Stir in the club soda with a swizzle stick and enjoy.

# 79.  Lavender Lemonade

**Preparation Time:** 10 minutes

**Servings:** 6

**Cooking Time:** 40 minutes

**Ingredients:**

- 1 tbsp. dried lavender flowers
- 1 c. regular sugar
- 2 c. water
- 1 ½ c. lemon juice
- 2 c. cold water
- Ice cubes as per requirement
- Lime slices to garnish

**Directions:**

- Boil the two cups of water. Separate the stems from the lavender leaves.
- Place the lavender flowers in a jug or a bowl and add the sugar to it.
- Pour in the hot boiling water and give it a good stir. Make sure you stir till the sugar melts and dissolves.
- Cover the jug or bowl and set it aside for at least half an hour.

- Strain the infused water and pour it into your mixing pitcher.
- Pour in the lime juice and chilled water and mix. Fill your serving glasses with ice cubes and pour in the lavender lemonade.
- Add lime slices to garnish and serve chilled.

# 80. Raspberry-Cranberry Twist

**Preparation Time:** 10 minutes

**Servings:** 2

**Ingredients:**

- 12 oz. orange-flavored soda/carbonated beverage
- 12 oz. cranberry-raspberry juice

**Directions:**

- Mix the orange-orange soda with cranberry-raspberry juice. Pour it over ice.
- Serve.

# 81. Rhubarb Citrus

**Preparation Time:** 10 minutes

**Servings:** 6

**Ingredients:**

- 2 c. rhubarb juice
- 2 lemons, juiced
- ¼ c. simple syrup
- 1 ½ c. sparkling water
- Ice cubes for serving
- Mint leaves for garnish
- Edible flowers for garnish

**Directions:**

- Combine the rhubarb juice, lemon juice, syrup, and sparkling water in a pitcher. Chill for 2 hours.

- Spoon the ice cubes into serving glasses and pour the drink over them.

- Garnish with mint leaves and edible flowers. Serve immediately.

# 82.   Kiwi Mojito Mocktail

**Preparation Time:** 10 minutes

**Servings:** 2

**Ingredients:**

- 1 lemon juice

- 2 peeled and chopped kiwis

- 4-5 mint leaves

- 3 tbsps. honey

- 2 c. soda water

- Ice cubes for serving

**Directions:**

- Add the lemon juice, kiwis, and mint leaves to a pitcher. Use a muddler to crush the ingredients a little.

- Top with honey and soda water. Cover the pitcher with plastic wrap and chill for 2 hours.

- Spoon the ice cubes into serving glasses and top them with the drink.

- Serve immediately.

# 83. Orange Eggnog Mocktail

**Preparation Time:** 10 minutes

**Servings:** 4

**Ingredients:**

- A pack of 175 grams of concentrated orange juice
- 240 ml of ready-made eggnog without alcohol
- 240 ml of water
- 1 tsp. vanilla
- 70 grams of sugar
- A pinch of grated nutmeg, ice, and whipped cream

**Directions:**

- Put all the ingredients in a blender, starting with the eggnog and the water. Blend on high speed for 2 minutes.
- Put the mixture in the glasses and garnish with whipped cream and nutmeg.

# 84. Kombucha Grapefruit Agua Fresca

**Preparation Time:** 10 minutes

**Servings:** 4

**Ingredients:**

- 1 c. grapefruit juice
- 1 c. unflavored kombucha
- 1 tsp. honey
- 2 fresh rosemary sprigs
- ½ c. sparkling water

**Directions:**

- In a pitcher, combine the grapefruit juice, kombucha, honey, rosemary sprigs, and sparkling water.

- Chill for 2 hours.
- Pour the drink into serving glasses.
- Serve.

# 85.　Lime Zinger Mocktail

**Preparation Time:** 10 minutes

**Servings:** 4

**Ingredients:**

- 1 small cucumber, cut into strips
- 1 lime, cut into thin slices
- Ice cubes
- 3 c. white grape juice
- 1 ½ c. lime-flavored sparkling water

**Directions:**

- In a pitcher, add all the ingredients and mix well.
- Pour the drink into serving glasses and serve immediately.

# 86.　Mango Margarita Mocktail

**Preparation Time:** 10 minutes

**Servings:** 4

**Ingredients:**

- 6 tbsps. fresh mango puree
- ½ lemon, juiced
- 4 tbsps. simple syrup
- 2 c. sparkling water
- Ice cubes for serving
- Fresh mint leaves for serving

**Directions:**

- Mix the mango puree, lemon juice, syrup, and sparkling water in a pitcher.
- Spoon ice cubes into serving glasses and top them with the drink.
- Garnish with the mint leaves and serve immediately.

# 87.  Mint Julep Mocktail

**Preparation Time:** 60 minutes

**Ingredients:**

- ¼ c. filtered water
- ¼ c. white sugar
- 1 tbsp. fresh, chopped mint leaves
- 2 c. crushed ice
- ½ c. ready-made orangeade
- Fresh sprigs of mint for garnish

**Directions:**

- Combine filtered water, white sugar, and one tablespoon of chopped mint leaves. Stir, and bring to a boil.
- Cook mixture until sugar is dissolved. Remove from heat. Set aside for cooling.
- After an hour or so, strain the mint leaves out.
- Fill two cups with crushed ice. Add half orangeade to each cup. Top with a splash of sugar syrup.
- Garnish cups with a straw and a sprig of mint.

- Serve.

# 88.  Cherry Limeade

**Preparation Time:** 10 minutes

**Servings:** 4

**Ingredients:**

- 6 tbsps. tart cherry juice concentrate (see note)
- 3 c. water or lemon-lime soda
- 1 c. fresh lime juice (12 to 14 limes)
- 1 to 2 c. sugar (to taste)
- Maraschino cherries (garnish; optional)

**Directions:**

- Mix cherry juice concentrate and water (or soda) in a large pitcher. Stir well to combine. Add lime juice and stir.
- Add sugar, beginning with ½ cup and adding more until desired sweetness is reached.
- Serve over ice, garnished with maraschino cherries if desired.

Note: Concentrated cherry juice can be found in the refrigerated juice aisle in most supermarkets. If you can't find any, you may substitute one packet of black cherry powdered drink mix. Prepare as directed on the packet, substituting soda for water if desired, then blend in lime juice and extra sugar if desired.

# 89.    Guava Watermelon and Lime Icy

**Preparation Time:** 5 hours, 20 minutes

**Servings:** 3

**Ingredients:**

- ½ seedless watermelon, chopped
- 1 ½ c. guava juice
- ¼ c. lime juice
- 2 tbsps. caster sugar
- Mint and lime to serve in glasses

**Directions:**

- In a blender, blitz the melon till smooth.
- Add guava, sugar, and lime.
- Freeze till almost frozen.
- Stir up and pour into glasses.
- Add mint and lime…sip!

# 90.    Mango and Strawberry Joy

**Preparation Time:** 10 minutes

**Servings:** 3

**Ingredients:**

- 1 packet of frozen strawberries and mango
- 3 c. milk
- 1 c. frozen yogurt
- ⅓ c. honey
- 1 c. crushed ice

**Directions:**

- In a blender, blitz all ingredients except ice.

- When it is smooth and creamy–pour over iced frosted glasses.
- Cheers!

# 91. Lime and Mint Melody

**Preparation Time:** 10 minutes

**Servings:** 8

**Ingredients:**

- 8 limes, quartered
- ⅔ c. fresh mint leave, chopped
- ½ c. lime cordial
- 2 c. ice, crushed
- 1 bottle of soda water, chilled

**Directions:**

- In a jug, combine mint and lime.
- Smash with the end of a wooden spoon.
- Pour in cordial and ice.
- Stir well.
- Top with soda and serve.

# 92.   Mango Madness

**Preparation Time:** 10 minutes

**Servings:** 4

**Ingredients:**

- 4 c. mango, chopped
- 1 can of coconut milk
- 2 c. coconut water
- ½ c. caster sugar
- Ice

**Directions:**

- In a blender, combine mango and sugar.
- Blitz till smooth.
- Pour in water and milk with ice.
- Blitz till creamy.
- Pour into frosted glasses and serve up fresh.

# 93.   Lime Cola

**Preparation Time:** 10 minutes

**Servings:** 36

**Ingredients:**

- Ice cubes
- Cola
- ½ lemon, juiced
- Lemon slices, for garnish

**Directions:**

- Fill a highball glass with ice
- Fill with cola and juice of ½ lime

# 94.   Roy Rogers

**Preparation Time:** 10 minutes

**Servings:** 3

**Ingredients:**

- Ice cubes
- Cola
- Grenadine
- Cherry or lemon

**Directions:**

- Fill a highball glass with ice
- Fill with cola
- Splash of grenadine
- Garnish with cherry or lemon

# 95.   Passion Fruit Martini Mocktail

**Preparation Time:** 10 minutes

**Servings:** 2

**Ingredients:**

- ½ c. passion fruit juice
- 1 oz. Lemon juice
- 1 oz. Egg white
- 1 oz. Simple syrup
- Ice
- Sparkling grape juice
- Slice of lime for garnish

**Directions:**

- Into a shaker, add the passion fruit juice, lemon juice, egg white, and simple syrup and give it a dry shake for 15 seconds.
- Add the ice, then shake again until the outside of the shaker feels cold.
- Double strain into a martini glass.
- Top it with the grape juice and top some foam left on the shaker.
- Garnish with a slice of lime.
- Enjoy!

# 96.   Passion Fruit Mocktail

**Preparation Time:** 10 minutes

**Servings:** 2

**Ingredients:**

- 4 passion fruits
- 2.5 oz. Simple syrup
- Soda water
- Ice
- Rosemary spring for garnish

**Directions:**

- Take the passion fruit inside and put it into a blender.
- Add the simple syrup.
- Pulse for about 1 minute until the fruit is completely blended.

- Put ice cubes in a glass.

- Strain some of the mixtures.

- Top off with soda water.

- Add a rosemary spring.

- Enjoy!

# 97. Piña Colada

**Preparation Time:** 10 minutes

**Servings:** 2

**Ingredients:**

- 1 oz. Mango syrup

- 2 oz. Coconut milk

- 1 oz. Apple juice

- ½ c. pineapple fruit (slices)

- Ice cubes

**Directions:**

- Pour all ingredients into a blender, then add some ice cubes.

- Blend until smooth.

- Pour the mix into a glass.

- Garnish with a slice of pineapple and a spring of mint.

- Enjoy!

# 98.    Sparkling Peach Punch

**Preparation Time:** 10 minutes

**Servings:** 2

**Ingredients:**

- 3 c. brewed green tea
- 5 large ripe peaches
- 1 oz. Lime juice
- 5 c. ginger ale
- 2 oz. Agave nectar
- 5-7 mint leaves

**Directions:**

- Blend four peaches and lime juice until smooth.
- In a pitcher, add ice, one peach into slices, the peach juice, green tea, and agave nectar.
- Top it with ginger ale and add mint leaves.
- Stir well.
- Enjoy!

# 99.  Strawberry Bellini Mocktail

**Preparation Time:** 10 minutes

**Servings:** 2

**Ingredients:**

- 4 to 6 large fresh strawberries
- 1 oz. Lime juice
- 20 ml strawberry syrup
- 20 ml simple syrup
- Soda water
- Ice cubes
- One-half strawberry for garnish

**Directions:**

- Put the strawberry, strawberry syrup, simple syrup, lime juice, and ice cubes into a blender.
- Blend until smooth.
- Pour blended ingredients into a chilled glass.
- Top with soda water.
- Garnish with a strawberry.
- Enjoy!

# 100.  Zucchini Mocktail

**Preparation Time:** 10 minutes

**Servings:** 2

**Ingredients:**

- 4 oz. Zucchini juice
- 1 oz. Raw honey
- 1 oz. Lemon juice
- Ice cubes
- Zucchini or cucumber wheel for garnish

**Directions:**

- Blend zucchini with water (2:1 ratio).
- Strain through a fine-mesh strainer.
- Pour all ingredients into the shaker, including the ice.
- Shake well and strain into chilled glass.
- Garnish.
- Enjoy!

# Chapter 9: Frozen Recipes

## 101. Cold Brew Julep

**Preparation Time:** 3 minutes

**Servings:** 3

**Ingredients:**

- 10 mint leaves
- Crushed ice
- ½ oz. simple syrup
- 3 oz. Cold brew strong coffee

**Directions:**

- In a rocks glass, muddle 5 of the mint leaves.
- Add some crushed ice.
- Next, add the simple syrup along with the coffee and stir to combine.
- Garnish with remaining leaves and serve.

# 102. Fig and Vanilla Seltzers

**Preparation Time:** 10 minutes

**Servings:** 3

**Ingredients:**

- Juice of ½ a lemon
- 2 tbsp fig preserves
- 1 tbsp granulated sugar
- 4 oz. vanilla seltzer water

**Directions:**

- In a small bowl, stir together the lemon juice, fig preserves, and granulated sugar.
- Strain the mixture equally into two glasses.
- Pour 2 ounces of seltzer into each glass. Give each a quick stir with a straw to combine.
- Serve straight away!

# 103. Beach Punch

**Preparation Time:** 10 minutes

**Servings:** 3

**Ingredients:**

- 4 oz. Lemon soda
- 2 oz. Lemonade
- 1 oz. Pomegranate juice
- 2 oz. Strawberries, sliced
- ½ Mangoes, cubed
- 1 Strawberry fruit popsicle (optional)
- 1 Mango fruit popsicle (optional)

**Directions:**

- In a blender, add mangoes and strawberries and blend until a smooth puree is made.
- Separate the juice using a strainer
- Pour the juice into the serving glass with lemon soda, lemonade, and pomegranate juice.
- Mix well.
- Garnish, putting one popsicle inside the glass.
- Serve cold and enjoy.

# 104. Icy Arnold Palmer

**Preparation Time:** 10 minutes

**Servings:** 4

**Ingredients:**

- 4 single-serving size bags of black tea
- 4 c. boiling water
- 1 c. water
- 1 c. sugar
- 1 c. fresh lemon juice (8 to 10 large lemons)
- 2 c. crushed ice

**Directions:**

- In a heat-safe pitcher, pour boiling water over tea bags and allow to steep for 5 minutes. Place in refrigerator.
- In a medium saucepan, combine 1 cup of water and sugar; cook over medium heat until sugar is dissolved. Cool completely.
- Add sugar syrup, lemon juice, and ice to a blender; process until a slushie consistency is reached.
- Remove pitcher from refrigerator; add lemonade slush mixture and stir to combine. Taste and add more sugar if desired. Serve immediately.

Note: To serve a crowd, you can prepare our southern iced tea and classic lemonade recipes and combine them in a punch bowl or several large pitchers.

# 105. Peach Bellini Mocktail

**Preparation Time:** 10 minutes

**Servings:** 3

**Ingredients:**

- 1 Peach, sliced
- 4 oz. Apple juice
- ¼ oz. Sugar
- ½ oz. Lime juice

**Directions:**

- Make sure you use a frozen, sliced peach.
- In a blender jug, add apple juice, sugar, and lime juice.
- Blend it well.
- Add in the frozen peach slices and blend again until it is smooth.
- Pour out into the serving glass.
- Garnish with a peach slice on top for serving and enjoy.

# 106. Purple Mocktail

**Preparation Time:** 10 minutes

**Servings:** 3

## Ingredients:

- 3 Mint leaves
- 3 Blueberries
- 1 Lemon wheel
- 4 oz. Red bull purple, sugar-free
- 4 oz. Lemonade
- Ice as required

## Directions:

- Take the serving glass and add mint, blueberries, lemon wheel, and ice.
- Stir a little using a spoon
- Now, add red bull and lemonade.
- Stir again.
- Serve cool and enjoy.

# 107. Raspberry Lime Fizz

**Preparation Time:** 10 minutes

**Servings:** 4

## Ingredients:

- 1 c. raspberries, fresh or frozen, thawed if frozen

- Additional 1 c. raspberries, frozen
- ¾ c. sugar
- 5 c. (40 oz.) of cold club soda
- ½ c. fresh lime juice (9 to 10 limes)
- Crushed ice

**Directions:**

- Process raspberries in a blender until pureed; strain to remove seeds and pulp.
- Combine raspberry juice, sugar, club soda, and lime juice in a pitcher. Stir to combine; taste and add more sugar if desired.
- Serve over ice, spooning a few frozen raspberries into each glass.

# 108. Watermelon-Lime Slushie

**Preparation Time:** 10 minutes

**Servings:** 4

**Ingredients:**

- 3 c. chopped fresh watermelon
- 1 tbsp. sugar or natural sugar substitute
- 1 c. crushed or shaved ice
- 2 tbsps. fresh lime juice (1 to 2 limes)
- ½ c. water or lemon-lime soda
- Watermelon wedges; garnish; optional

**Directions:**

- Place all ingredients in a blender and process until smooth. Taste, adjust sugar and lime juice if desired, and serve immediately, garnished with watermelon wedges if desired.

# 109. Rosemary Mint Lemonade

**Preparation Time:** 10 minutes

**Servings:** 4

**Ingredients:**

- ½ c. sugar
- ½ c. water
- 2 tbsps. fresh rosemary leaves
- 2 tbsps. fresh mint leaves
- 1 c. fresh lemon juice (8 to 10 large lemons)
- 3 c. water
- Additional fresh rosemary and mint (for garnish; optional)

**Directions:**

- In a small saucepan over medium heat, combine sugar, herbs, and water until sugar is dissolved. Set aside to cool.
- When the mixture has cooled, strain out the herbs. Place in a pitcher with lemon juice and water; stir well to combine. Add more water or sugar to taste, if desired. Serve over ice, garnished with fresh herbs if desired.

# 110. Jet Set

**Preparation Time:** 10 minutes

**Servings:** 4

**Ingredients:**

- 6 cl cucumber juice (leave the peels)
- 1.5 cl fresh lime juice
- 1.5 cl agave nectar
- 5 basil leaves

**Directions:**

- Mix the basil leaves in a baking dish.
- Add the other ingredients. Shake with ice.
- Strain through a tea strainer with fresh ice.
- Peel the cucumber. Garnish with cucumber ribbons.

# 111. Cherry Lime Spritz

**Preparation Time:** 10 minutes

**Servings:** 4

**Ingredients:**

- 2 lime wedges
- 2 tbsp. Freshly squeezed lime juice
- 2 tbsp. 100% cherry juice
- 2 tbsp. Simple syrup (or 4 drops of liquid stevia, or to taste)
- ¾ c. your favorite sparkling water
- Additional lime wedges for garnish (optional)

**Directions:**

- Put two lime wedges in the bottom of the glass. Destroy the wedges with a jumbled tool.
- Add lime juice, cherry juice, and the sweetener of your choice, and mix up more.
- Pour carbonated water into the glass.
- Add a few ice cubes. Garnish with additional lime wedges if desired.

# 112. Cranberry Mocktail

**Preparation Time:** 10 minutes

**Servings:** 4

**Ingredients:**

- 1 c. crushed ice
- 1 c. cranberry kombucha *
- ½ c. pomegranate juice
- ½ c. freshly squeezed orange juice

**Directions:**

- Pour all the ingredients into a serving glass and mix until well blended.

Kombucha is not technically alcohol-free, as the fermentation process creates an exceedingly small amount of alcohol. If you prefer a 100% soft drink, replace the kombucha with ginger beer or another flavored soda.

# 113. Mint Matcha Chiller

**Preparation Time:** 10 minutes

**Servings:** 4

**Ingredients:**

- 12 cl chilled sparkling water
- 4–5 mint leaves, chopped
- 1 tsp. lemon juice
- 1 tsp. Matcha green tea powder

**Directions:**

- Pour all the ingredients into a serving glass. Mix until combined.

# 114. Cold Coffee Mocktail

**Preparation Time:** 10 minutes

**Servings:** 4

**Ingredients:**

- ¾ c. coconut cream
- ¾ c. cold coffee
- 4 tsp birch xylitol
- ½ tsp. Almond extract
- 1 tbsp. Raw cocoa powder
- Unsweetened chocolate flakes and coconut whipped cream for garnish

**Directions:**

- Pour all the ingredients into a serving glass. Blend until combined.
- Top with unsweetened chocolate chips and coconut whipped cream.

# 115. Mocktail Chai

**Preparation Time:** 10 minutes

**Servings:** 4

**Ingredients:**

- ½ c. turmeric almond juice
- ½ c. Ceylon tea
- ½ tsp. Almond extract
- ¾ c. cream or coconut cream
- Cinnamon stick

**Directions:**

- Pour all the ingredients into a serving glass. Mix until combined.
- Garnish with a cinnamon stick.

# 116. Ginger Mojito

**Preparation Time:** 10 minutes

**Servings:** 4

**Ingredients:**

- 200 ml of ginger soda
- 30 ml of lime juice
- 30 ml of simple syrup
- 10 mint leaves and some
- Sprig to decorate
- 1 lime wedge to decorate

**Directions:**

- Press the mint leaves in a shaker, add the syrup and lime juice, then some ice, and shake well. Top with ginger soda, then strain and serve in a glass of ice. Garnish with a sprig of mint and a wedge of lime.

# 117. Lemon with Coconut

**Preparation Time:** 10 minutes

**Servings:** 4

**Ingredients:**

- ½ c. coconut water
- ½ c. tonic water, chilled
- 1 tbsp. Lime juice
- Pinch of rosemary for garnish
- Lime zest for garnish

**Directions:**

- Pour all the ingredients into a serving glass. Mix until combined.
- Garnish with spiral lime, rosemary, and lime zest.

# 118. Pomegranate Twist

**Preparation Time:** 10 minutes

**Servings:** 4

**Ingredients:**

- ½ c. sparkling water
- ¼ c. pomegranate juice com
- Ice
- Orange zest for garnish

**Directions:**

- In a glass, add ice and pour all the ingredients.
- Mix and garnish with a fresh orange twist.

# 119. Pomegranate-Lemon Spritzer

**Preparation Time:** 10 minutes

**Servings:** 4

**Ingredients:**

- 1 bottle (16 oz.) of pomegranate juice
- 1 (2-litre) bottle of club soda, unflavored sparkling water, or lemon-lime soda
- 1 c. fresh lemon juice (8 to 10 large lemons)
- ½ to ¾ c. sugar (to taste)

**Directions:**

- In a large pitcher, combine pomegranate juice, lemon juice, and enough water or soda to fill the pitcher. Add sugar one tablespoonful at a time, frequently tasting, until desired sweetness is reached (see note).
- Serve immediately, over ice if desired.

Note: You may find that this drink is sweet enough without added sugar, especially if you use lemon-lime soda.

# 120. Red Moon

**Preparation Time:** 10 minutes

**Servings:** 4

**Ingredients:**

- 180 ml of carbonated water
- 60 ml of plum-cinnamon shrub
- Plum slices to decorate

**Directions:**

- Mix the shrub with the carbonated water in a glass filled with ice and mix well. Garnish with plum slices.

# 121. Sun Mocktail

**Preparation Time:** 10 minutes

**Servings:** 4

**Ingredients:**

- 1 sprig of mint and a lime wedge to decorate
- 60 ml of lime juice
- ½ tsp. molasses
- 240 ml of ginger soda

**Directions:**

- Mix all the ingredients in a large glass filled with crushed ice, pouring in the molasses first, then the ginger soda, and finally the lime juice. Garnish with the lime wedge and mint.

# 122. Thai Mango Iced Tea

**Preparation Time:** 10 minutes

**Servings:** 4

**Ingredients:**

- 2 tsps. cashew drink
- 2 tsps. condensed milk
- 2 tsps. Granulated sugar
- ½ tsp. molasses
- 1 bag of Thai black tea
- 240 ml of boiling water

- 4 slices of dehydrated mango and a few more are cut into thin strips to decorate

**Directions:**

- In a large cup or bowl, steep the tea, mango, and sugar in hot water, then allow cooling. Remove the mango and the tea bag. Add the remaining ingredients and mix. Serve in a large glass filled with ice cubes and garnish with thin mango strips.

# 123. Trini Tea

**Preparation Time:** 10 minutes

**Servings:** 4

**Ingredients:**

- 9 cl coffee
- 4.5 cl coconut milk
- 1.5 cl cascara tea syrup
- Aromatic macaroons
- Angostura bitter orange

**Directions:**

- Pour the two hot cups of coffee into the shaker together with all the other ingredients, shake

# 124. Honeycrisp Cooler

**Preparation Time:** 10 minutes

**Servings:** 4

**Ingredients:**

- 6 cl Honeycrisp fresh apple juice
- 1.5 cl ginger syrup *
- 1.5 cl fresh lemon juice
- 9 cl tonic water

**Directions:**

- Add all the ingredients to a serving glass with ice.

- Mix, garnish with an apple slice, and serve.
- Preparation of ginger syrup:
- Combine the water and ginger in a pan. Bring to a boil.
- Once boiling, stir the sugar slowly until completely dissolved.
- Reduce the heat. Boil for 20 minutes.
- Let it cool down. Filter the ginger before use.

# Chapter 10: Holidays Recipes

## 125. Strawberry Faux Daiquiri

**Preparation Time:** 10 minutes

**Servings:** 2

**Ingredients:**

- 2 strawberries (large)
- 1 ½ pt. Lemonade ice (crushed).

For garnishing:

- 1 small strawberry

**Directions:**

- Hull strawberries.
- Blend the lemonade, crushed ice, and strawberries in a blender.
- Mix ingredients. Combine ingredients in a glass.

- Use strawberries for garnish.
- Serve.

# 126. Caramel Apple Mocktail

**Preparation Time:** 10 minutes

**Servings:** 2

**Ingredients:**

- ½ c. caramel apple Syrup
- 6 c. Cider
- 2 tsp. ground cinnamon
- Apples
- 7 sprigs rosemary
- 3 c. sparkling water
- To rim a glass: brown sugar

**Directions:**

- Combine caramel syrup, apple cider, and cinnamon in a pitcher.
- Cut the apples into thin slices and add them to the pitcher. Add rosemary sprigs. Allow to sit for approximately 20 minutes.
- Mix well.
- Dip the glass rims in brown sugar.
- Serve mocktails in sugar-rimmed glasses.

# 127. Berry Shrub

**Preparation Time:** 10 minutes

**Servings:** 2

**Ingredients:**

- 2 c. rinsed, drained, crushed blackberries (or 2 c., fresh, rinsed)
- 2 c. sugar, white

Optional:

- 2 thyme sprigs
- 2 sage sprigs
- 1 c. white vinegar

**Directions:**

- Wash and then sterilize the jars or bowls.
- Add the blackberries to the bowl and then cover them with white sugar. Add the thyme and sage.
- Combine by stirring.
- Cover the jar with cling wrap. Keep in the refrigerator for at least one to two days. Stir occasionally until you get a thick syrup or juice around the berries.
- Take out thyme and sage sprigs.
- Use a fine strainer to strain the blackberry mixture into a separate bowl. Place the blackberry mixture into a bowl.
- Sterilize a glass jar or bottle. Add vinegar and juice. Cover and give sugar a gentle shake to dissolve completely.
- Let the flavors rest for at least one day. Serve.

# 128. Appletini

**Preparation Time:** 10 minutes

**Servings:** 2

**Ingredients:**

- ¼ fluid oz. lemon juice (fresh if available)
- ½ oz. simple syrup (pre-bottled)
- 2 fluid oz. 2 fluid oz.

For Dipping Rim:

- Sugar, white
- For garnishing:
- 1 slice of apple

**Directions:**

- Fill a Mocktail shaker with ice.
- Mix the syrup, lemon juice, and apple juice in a shaker.
- Strain into a sugar-rimmed glass.
- Serve with a slice of apple.

# 129.  Spook Lights

**Preparation Time:** 10 minutes

**Servings:** 2

**Ingredients:**

- Tonic water
- Grenadine syrup (or any flavoring syrup)
- Blacklight

**Directions:**

- Fill the glass with tonic water.
- Add about ⅓ as much grenadine syrup (to taste).
- Turn off the lights and place them by UV or black light. Serve.

# 130.  Severe Hand in the Punch

**Preparation Time:** 10 minutes

**Servings:** 2

**Ingredients:**

**Makes:** 2 hands

- Water
- 2 rubber gloves
- Food coloring (optional)
- 1 bowl of your favorite punch

**Directions:**

- Fill the rubber gloves with water, then squirt in some food coloring. Tie a knot in the top, shake (to mix up the food coloring), then lay flat on a baking tray.
- Place in the freezer until frozen, about 3 hours. Carefully cut the gloves off. Place the frozen hand into your punch bowl with your favorite punch. When it melts, place the second one in.

# 131.  Sparkling Ginger

**Preparation Time:** 10 minutes

**Servings:** 2

**Ingredients:**

- Juice from 3 small oranges (about 1 c. orange juice)
- 1 oz. lemon juice
- Juice from 1 medium grapefruit (1 c. grapefruit juice)
- Juice from 2 mall blood oranges (about ½ c. blood orange juice)
- 2 oz. lime juice
- 1 ½ oz. ginger juice
- Kosher salt
- Honey syrup
- Chilled sparkling mineral water

**Directions:**

- Juice your ginger and fruits in a juicer and combine them. Place in a refrigerator to chill until serving time.
- Include about ½ cup of ginger citrusade in a glass and top with ice to assemble. Include about one tablespoon of honey syrup (according to your desired sweetness, you can also add more)
- Add about a pinch of salt and ½ mineral water. Stir to mix well, and use any citrus slice to garnish
- You might want to leave out the pinch of salt but don't, as it would be vital to the drink. The purpose of the salt is to get the flavors of the citrus more prominent, and it makes the drink taste better overall
- In an airtight container, store your mixed juices for up to 3 days in the refrigerator
- To prepare the honey syrup, allow a half cup of filtered water to boil and include about 1 cup of honey. Stir the mixture so the honey blends and leave to cool and come to room temperature. At room temperature, keep in an airtight container.

# 132. Hibiscus Pineapple Mocktail

**Preparation Time:** 10 minutes

**Servings:** 2

**Ingredients:**

- ¼ c. sugar
- ¼ c. dried hibiscus petals

- 2 fresh cilantro sprigs
- 2-inch piece of fresh ginger
- 2 ¼ c. water
- ½ fresh pineapple (should be peeled then cored)

**Directions:**

- Start by peeling the ginger, then chop it into very thin pieces. Use the end of the knife that was used to chop to smash the ginger pieces. Add ginger to a small saucepan. Add about ¼ cup of water and sugar to the saucepan and let it come to a boil.
- Reduce the heat, cover, and leave for 10 minutes to simmer. When the time is up, you will find it very aromatic. Allow to sit.
- You then want to add 2 cups of water to a pan and allow it to boil. When it boils, put off the heat and include the hibiscus petals. Leave to soak for 15 minutes covered. You'll want to be wary about where this mix touches, which will stain any surface.
- Strain the mixture and leave to cool
- In the meantime, use a blender to blend the pineapple or juice with a juicer, then strain. If you don't have the time to juice your pineapple, you can always buy pineapple juice
- You'll want to sieve the ginger out of the mixture of syrup and then distribute it among two glasses. Include a lot of ice cubes in the tall glasses. Equally, divide hibiscus and pineapple juice tea.
- Use the side of your knife to get cilantro sprigs bruised, then include them in the glass.
- You can scale this recipe depending on how many people will be served. You just have to double or triple the ingredients used.

# 133. Mint Lemongrass Mocktail

**Preparation Time:** 10 minutes

**Servings:** 2

**Ingredients:**

- 1 c. water
- 1 c. fresh mint (should be chopped roughly)
- Slices of mint and lime to garnish
- 2 lemongrass stalks
- 1 c. sugar
- Sparkling water

**Directions:**

- Cut off the bottoms and tops of your lemongrass and then out the sturdy outer part of the leaves to get to the softer insides.
- Slice this into pieces of 2 inches and use a rolling pin to bruise (you can also use any kind of heavy item available)
- In a small saucepan, add lemongrass, water, and sugar. Allow to come to a boil on medium heat and take away from the heat. Include mint leaves and allow to soak for about 15 minutes
- Strain the lemongrass and mint out of the tea keep, and it cool in an airtight container.

- Add about 1-2 tablespoons of syrup and ice to a glass. Include slices of lime, sparkling water, and mint in a glass

The syrup is made when 2 of these things are mixed with a 1-to-1 ratio of water and sugar. The preparation is simple – you only have to stir the sugar and hot water so the sugar dissolves. It is used mainly in iced coffee and Mocktails, but it's also a great addition when making mocktails.

# 134. Blueberry Peach Mocktail

**Preparation Time:** 10 minutes

**Servings:** 2

**Ingredients:**

- ½ c. fresh mint (with extra to garnish)
- 3 c. white grape juice
- ¼ c. organic apple cider vinegar
- 2 c. blueberries
- 2 peaches (should be sliced)
- 3 c. seltzer water

**Directions:**

- Add mint and ½ cup of blueberries into a drinking glass. Mash mint and blueberries to release juice so the mint is aromatic and the blueberries crushed. Add this blend to a large jug.
- Include the remaining blueberries in the jug, seltzer water, grape juice, apple cider vinegar, and peaches. Stir to get them well mixed.
- Put the jug in a refrigerator for about an hour to make the flavors prominent. Divide the drink into glasses when it is time to serve and use fresh mint to top.

# 135. Stone Fruit Mocktail

**Preparation Time:** 10 minutes

**Servings:** 2

**Ingredients:**

- ¾ c. raw light-colored honey
- ¾ c. apple cider vinegar
- Sparkling mineral water
- 1 lb. stone fruit (should be cut into chunks)
- 450g of yellow plums, white peaches, and white nectarines (should be cut into chunks
- 10 fresh thyme sprigs
- Crushed ice

**Directions:**

- Add the fruit into a glass bowl or a large mason jar. Include thyme leaves and honey, stir to mix well, then cover. Refrigerate for about until the fruit is like syrup or for 24 hours
- Strain this mixture with a fine mesh strainer. While straining, firmly press the fruit so you can amass as much syrup as possible.
- Add vinegar and stir, then transfer into a clean bottle or jar. Allow to sit for 24 hours in the fridge before using

- Add ice with some spoonfuls of syrup, then include sparkling water (it should be roughly about three parts sparkling water to 1 part syrup)

# 136. Virgin Mojito

**Preparation Time:** 10 minutes

**Servings:** 2

**Ingredients:**

- Small mint bunch
- Soda water
- 3 limes (should be juiced)
- 1 tbsp. sugar

**Directions:**

- Mash leaves mint leaves with sugar with a mortar and pestle (you can also use the end of a rolling pin and a small bowl)
- In 2 tall glasses, add a handful of crushed ice. Distribute the lime juice among the tall glasses along with the mint blend.
- Place a straw in and add soda water.

# 137. Thyme Grapefruit Syrup

**Preparation Time:** 10 minutes

**Servings:** 2

**Ingredients:**

- A handful of thyme leaves
- ¾ c. organic pure cane sugar
- 5 c. fresh water
- 2 large grapefruit strips of skin
- ¼ c. honey
- 1 c. pineapple juice
- Thyme leaves

- 1 c. grapefruit juice
- Sliced grapefruit

**Directions:**

- Add water to a medium pot over medium-high heat and allow it to come to a boil. When water boils, include the thyme leaves with the water and add grapefruit skin strips. Leave for 10 minutes to boil
- When time is up, put the heat off and add the honey with the pure cane sugar as you get the mixture covered. Leave for 27 – 30 minutes to let it soak so that the flavors are well incorporated.
- When fully soaked, take the thyme leaves and grapefruit out and transfer this into a medium jug and keep
- To prepare the mocktails, put crushed ice in glasses and use the syrup of grapefruit/thyme to fill about half of the glass. Also, add about ¼ of the grapefruit juice with pineapple juice.
- Top with thyme leaves and sliced grapefruits to garnish.
- Do this same process for the rest of the servings and enjoy
- You can store the grapefruit/thyme mixture for up to 1 week in a tightly sealed jar in the fridge.
- Rather than add the honey and pure cane sugar, you can still just use 1 cup of honey to get a more delicate taste.

# 138. Basil Lemongrass Mocktail

**Preparation Time:** 10 minutes

**Servings:** 2

**Ingredients:**

- 2 c. granulated sugar
- 1 c. lemongrass (should be sliced thinly)
- ¼ c. sanding sugar
- 2 oz. fresh orange juice
- 4 oz. fresh lime juice
- 2 c. water
- 2 c. fresh Genovese basil leaves plus extra
- ¼ c. kosher salt
- 1 tbsp. orange zest
- 4 oz. double-strength brewed white tea
- Orange twists

**Directions:**

- Add sugar, lemongrass, water, and basil to a medium saucepan and allow to come to a boil. When boiling, remove the saucepan from the heat and leave the mixture to soak for about 2 hours.
- When time is up, strain the mixture and leave it to chill. You can also make the syrup way before you want to make your mocktail, which can be stored in the fridge until needed.
- Add salt, sanding sugar, and orange zest to a plate or shallow bowl and combine. Use a wedge of lime, orange, or lemon to slightly moisten the rims of 2 large glasses. Push the rims of the glasses into the mixture of sugar
- Pour into a Mocktail shaker white tea, lime juice, 3 ounces of simple syrup, and orange juice and muddle. Add ice to the mixture and shake well.
- Add regular ice or one large ice cube to your prepared glasses. Distribute the mixture between the glasses and use an orange twist basil spring to garnish.

# 139. New York Mocktail

**Preparation Time:** 10 minutes

**Servings:** 2

**Ingredients:**

- A couple of vanilla extract drops
- 3 tsps. maple syrup
- Ice
- 10 ml of pomegranate juice
- 1 tsp. Assam tea leaves
- 25 ml of lemon juice
- 1 tbsp. egg white

**Directions:**

- Boil 150 ml of water and pour it over the tea leaves. Stir well and immediately strain. The aim is not to get stewed tea but a strong one. Add the vanilla extract to the tea, mix and allow to cool.
- In a Mocktail shaker, add maple syrup, lemon juice, and 50 ml of the tea. Use a fork to loosen egg whites, then include about one tablespoon in the Mocktail shaker.
- Shake the Mocktail shaker well so that the mix is frothy. Use a handful of ice to top the mixture, then shake again.
- Fill a glass with ice and double-strain the mixture into it. Make your pomegranate juice 20 ml by adding water to it. Pour this into your glass slowly. Leave for some time to sit, and you should find the juice floating beneath the foam of egg white.

# 140. Negroni Mocktail

**Preparation Time:** 10 minutes

**Servings:** 2

**Ingredients:**

- 1 orange slice
- 3 pods of cardamom (should be crushed lightly)
- A couple of red food coloring drops
- ½ grapefruit
- 125g of caster sugar
- A pinch of coriander seeds
- 25 ml of white grape juice
- Ice

**Directions:**

- Cut the grapefruit into small pieces, then transfer it into a saucepan. Add sugar, orange slice, coriander seeds, cardamom pods, and 125 ml of water.
- Leave the mixture to heat till it simmers and cook for 5 minutes as you use the back of a wooden spoon to crush the pieces of fruit so that it discharges the juices.
- When the white pit is washed out and the fruit is softened, remove it from the heat and allow it to cool. You could also include the red food coloring during this time.
- After this mixture of syrup is cool, get it strained and dispose of the fruit pieces and spices. Use ice to fill a tumbler and add about 25 ml of the syrup mixture, 25 ml of cold water, and grape juice. Gently stir so you can feel the outer part of the tumbler getting cold.
- Use a slice of orange to garnish.

# 141. Agua Fresca

**Preparation Time:** 10 minutes

**Servings:** 2

**Ingredients:**

- 1 c. fresh pineapple chunks
- 3 limes (should be juices

- 1 c. frozen peach slices
- Limes slices to serve
- 3 ripe peaches (should be cubed and peeled0
- 2 c. water
- 2 tbsp. simple syrup
- Fresh mint

**Directions:**

- You'll want to combine equal parts of water and sugar to make a simple syrup. An example is ¼ cup of water and ¼ cup of sugar. Combine both in a saucepan over medium heat. Stir so that sugar completely dissolves, and leave for about 1 – 2 minutes to simmer. Take away from the heat and leave to cool.
- Include pineapple and peaches with 1 cup of water in a blender and combine so that it is thoroughly blended.
- Pour this blended mixture through a fine mesh sieve into a large measuring cup or bowl and press out the remainder of the mixture with a spoon towards the end.
- In a large jug, combine the lime juice, the rest of the water, syrup, and juice. You can add more syrup after tasting if you think it's needed, then chill in the fridge.
- Include the slices of frozen peach before you serve, as this would function as ice cubes. But if you would like it to be extra cold, you could still top it with more ice.
- Serve with mint and extra slices of lime

# 142. Raspberry Blackcurrant Mocktail

**Preparation Time:** 10 minutes

**Servings:** 2

**Ingredients:**

- Juice from half lime (you could use any other citrus)
- Fresh mint for garnishing
- 4 fresh raspberries
- 6 oz. Sparkling gourmet blackcurrant lime sparkling water (should be chilled)

**Directions:**

- Get 1 liter of cold water and use sparkling gourmet blackcurrant lime sparkling water to flavor.
- Muddle the raspberries in a serving glass and squeeze lime juice. Add ice in a glass and include the sparkling gourmet blackcurrant lime sparkling water.
- Stir to mix it well and use fresh mint and sliced lime to garnish.

# 143. Honey Mint Mocktail

**Preparation Time:** 10 minutes

**Servings:** 2

**Ingredients:**

- Handful of leaves
- ½ c. honey
- 2 – 3 c. water
- ½ c. lime juice (juice from about 4 limes)
- Mint leaves
- 1 c. juice from an orange
- Sliced limes

**Directions:**

- Start by adding water to a medium pot and letting it boil over medium-high heat. When it boils, include the mint leaves and leave for about 6 minutes to boil.
- Put off the heat after 6 minutes are up and add the honey. Stir the mixture, cover, and leave for 10 – 15 minutes to steep. This will make sure that the flavor of the mint is well incorporated.
- When it's been infused fully, remove the mint leaves and transfer them into a medium jug.
- In a glass, add crushed ice and use the mint/honey syrup to fill about half of the glass. Top with ¼ of the orange juice and about three tablespoons of lime juice. Add the mint leaves and sliced lime to the glass to garnish.
- Do this same process for the rest of the glasses.
- Enjoy!

# 144. Basil Strawberry Mocktail

**Preparation Time:** 10 minutes

**Servings:** 2

**Ingredients:**

- 1 c. organic pineapple juice
- A handful of basil leaves
- 2 c. strawberries (with the stems taken out, then should be sliced)
- 3 – 4 tbsps. agave syrup
- Ginger beer to top
- Sliced strawberries
- Crushed ice
- Fresh basil leaves

**Directions:**

- Add basil leaves, sliced strawberries, and pineapple juice to a bowl. Squash and mull the fruit and leaves together so that the basil leaves are somewhat crushed and the strawberries and completely broken down.
- Include the agave and stir so that it is well mixed. Depending on your desired sweetness, you can also include an extra sweetener.

- Add crushed ice and top with 3 tablespoons of crushed strawberries in glasses. Add ginger beer and about ⅓ cup of the mulled pineapple/strawberry mixture.
- You can use basil leaves and sliced strawberries to garnish. Do the same process for the rest of the servings.

# 145. Strawberry Watermelon Lime Mocktail

**Preparation Time:** 10 minutes

**Servings:** 2

**Ingredients:**

- 3 c. cubed watermelon
- 3 – 4 tbsps. agave syrup
- 2 c. strawberries (with the stems taken out, then should be sliced)
- 2 c. fresh water
- ¼ c. lime juice, freshly squeezed
- Lime wedges
- Cubed watermelon
- Fresh strawberries slices

**Directions:**

- Add watermelon, sliced strawberries, and lime juice to a bowl. Squash and mull the fruits and leaves together so that the watermelon and strawberries are entirely broken down.
- Include the agave and water and stir so that it is well mixed. Depending on your desired sweetness, you can also include an extra sweetener.
- Add crushed ice and top with three tablespoons of crushed strawberries/watermelon mix in glasses. To get the glasses about ¾ filled, add about ⅓ cup of the mocktail liquid mixture.
- You can add cubed watermelon, sliced strawberries, and lime wedges as garnish. Do the same process for the rest of the servings.
- Enjoy your drink.

To muddle the fruit, be sure to use a large bowl. The advantage of using a large bowl is that you get more space to mash and squash without the contents splashing.

# 146. Irish Cream Liqueur (Non-Alcoholic)

**Preparation Time:** 10 minutes

**Servings:** 2

**Ingredients:**

- 50 ml of evaporated milk
- 2 tbsps. maple syrup
- A pinch of ground cinnamon
- A pinch of orange zest, finely grated
- 150 ml of double cream
- 25 ml of espresso, freshly brewed
- 1 tsp. vanilla extract
- Ice

**Directions:**

- Add the ingredients to a large jug or Mocktail shaker. Include the ice liberally.
- Shake the Mocktail shaker well (if using) so that the outer part feels chilled. Pour into tumblers double strained.
- If you use a jug to combine, stir well so it is well mixed.
- Pour over ice and enjoy.

# Conclusion

Thank you for making it to the end!

You are now familiar with a good number of mocktail recipes. If you have tasted them all, you may refer to yourself as a bartender. If you've been exploring the recipes, you may have realized that making mocktails is as easy as falling asleep. Any juices could be blended and combined to create a custom mocktail. You could even name it if you want to..

There is absolutely no chance that anything could go wrong when making a mocktail. Knowing the formulas also makes it simple to make your own cocktails by substituting your preferred alcoholic beverage for soda or water. Even though it is straightforward, this cookbook is handy for making drinks.

There are a few essential bartending supplies. A shaker, sieve, jigger, and stirrer are required. Glassware will also be necessary. Highball, martini, and Collins glasses are all suitable options.

The game is different nowadays; people are more curious about flavors, so more care is taken to balance them. Additionally, concoctions have become more inventive, encouraging people to beg for more. Some folks who previously flavored alcohol-based mocktails have realized they don't need the booze because mocktails have grown to be so delicious. While other drink designers try to develop tastes from scratch, mocktails are reimaginings of sophisticated drinks with layers of flavors.

Your region's fruits and juices will have the biggest impact on the flavor of your mocktails. Otherwise, all you need to make them are common kitchen staples and equipment.

Making mocktails is not subject to any specific guidelines. As previously said, the appeal of creating mocktails is that you may play with them endlessly without utterly failing. You'll always have a nice beverage in your hand.

Enjoy your mocktail!

# Index

Made in United States
North Haven, CT
27 February 2023